Michael Fonseca
author of *Living in God's Embrace*

D1314814

LoViNG iN THE MASTER'S
footsteps

God's Dream for Us

ave maria press Notre Dame, Indiana

To Randall Becker,
true friend and spiritual companion,
whose life and example have helped me find God in life's daily
grind; whose steadfast faith has taught me patience and
endurance in loss and disappointment. To him this book, which
he so painstakingly edited and enriched, is dedicated with
affection and much joy.

Imprimatur: The Most Reverend Patrick R. Cooney
                  Bishop of Gaylord
Given at Gaylord, MI on 12 May 2003.

www.avemariapress.com

International Standard Book Number: 0-87793-994-2

Cover and text design by Katherine Robinson Coleman

Printed and bound in the United States of America.

Library of Congress Cataloging-in-Publication Data
Fonseca, Michael.
    Loving in the Master's footsteps : God's dream for us / Michael Fonseca.
        p. cm.
Includes bibliographical references.
    ISBN 0-87793-994-2 (pbk.)
    1. Spiritual life--Catholic Church. I. Title.

    BX2350.3.F66 2003
    248.4'82--dc21

                                                2003007336

CONTENTS

Preface
A View From Above

In writing this book, I have had in mind the many *serious* Christian seekers I have met in the course of giving retreats and workshops on prayer and spirituality. I am thinking as well of the many men and women I have been privileged to accompany in spiritual direction, either individually or in a group. In many instances, they had come to a significant crossroads in their relationship with God. Having traversed beyond the initial stages of prayer, they were no longer asking the questions a beginner generally asks: What do I have to do to become a more spiritual person? Who is God *for me?* Do I have a *personal* relationship with God? How *should* I pray? How do I know that God is *communicating* with me? Indeed, these individuals were seasoned enough to have received convincing answers to these and similar questions. Now they were moving toward new horizons on their journey.

The deeper questions were obviously being asked from the vantage point of greater intimacy with God. God had become a personal presence in their lives, to the point where their yearning for God was becoming a familiar awareness. They had embraced the fuller meaning of the words expressed by St John of the Cross:

> I live without living in myself,
> And I hope in such a way
> That I die because I am not dying.[1]

Daily prayer and the practice of God's presence during the day had become an essential ingredient of their lifestyle. These seekers had arrived at the third mansion of Saint Teresa of Avila's Interior Castle. Their commitment to God had become strong enough that they did not want to offend God deliberately even in small matters; and they had a deep concern that they would never revert to a state of dissipation and inconstancy.

Their life of intimacy with God had been strengthened and sustained by a powerful sense that God loved them unconditionally and had forgiven them all their sins. More importantly, God's forgiveness and mercy had set the stage for them to make a first hand experience of God's intense desire to share the divine life with them and offer them all the privileges and blessings of belonging to God's *very own* family. God's dream for them was beginning to be realized, and in response to the divine largesse, they wanted to give God their utmost in return. Their quest was now being encountered on a much deeper level, originating from that place in the heart where God was becoming absolute. They were now asking questions such as: Where do *You* want me to go? What do *You* want me to do with my life? How can I *best* serve You? What *more* can I give You?

In other words, the questions revolved around God being the center of their lives. Their major concern was the fulfillment of God's plan of salvation for the world and they wanted to play a significant role in working with God. The relationship with God had now moved to the level where the seeker was being invited to become a disciple, to follow closely in the footsteps of the Master, to put on his mind and heart, and to become the image of Christ. Daunting as this new becoming might seem, in the disciple's mind this transformation of self and the world is God's intimate desire and will. So not only is this change possible, it is accessible.

God's enthusiasm to fulfill the divine plan is contagious. As a result, the disciple plunges ahead in the task of renewal. Jesus is the Lord of the vineyard and the one responsible for a bountiful harvest. The disciple's task is to make the Master's dream his or her own, to offer full cooperation and unmitigated ownership, so that at harvest time there is genuine cause for rejoicing and celebration.

This book then is about discipleship, yours and mine. Christian discipleship is a wholehearted commitment to Jesus, resulting in a lifestyle that patterns itself on the teachings and power of the Savior. Slowly and inexorably, God becomes the *one and only true* Absolute. Discipleship, therefore, centers on your relationship and life with God and the progressive transformation that takes place in you because you are now residing in God's heart. Such is God's victorious plan for you and me. It is God's Pentecost dream for us brought to fulfillment in Jesus and proclaimed by the

Holy Spirit. This dream for us has been realized because the initiative has been God's *exclusively*. There was, therefore, never any chance of its failure.

THE BOOK'S FORMAT

How to Use This Manual

In some ways this book is a sequel to *Living in God's Embrace*, in that the first set of questions referred to in the Preface were addressed in that book. The expectation is that this book will continue the good work begun by the Holy Spirit in the hearts of the readers in the first book. Here, too, I have chosen a retreat format. Ultimately, true discipleship occurs when one sits for long periods of time at the feet of the Master. A retreat format is conducive to creating the habit of becoming like Mary who chose to sit at the feet of her Master (Lk 10:38–41). Every chapter begins with a conference about a select topic that will be the focus for prayer in that chapter. The ten prayer exercises that follow in each chapter have been designed to help the disciple deepen his or her own insights and graces. It might be helpful to read the whole book first, from beginning to end, as a way of getting the total picture, before you begin to use it as a manual of prayer and spiritual formation.

The topics discussed in the six chapters follow the dynamics of discipleship as outlined in the Old and New Testaments. God always initiates discipleship through a personal call to the individual. As a result, the individual is set apart for God, to do God's work and establish God's reign in the hearts of humankind. The disciple is progressively transformed as he or she works in close proximity with God who is always initiating the change. In remaining faithful to the conversion process, you will invariably deepen both your understanding of and commitment to being a disciple of Jesus.

The first chapter sets the stage for an understanding of Christian discipleship. In the Book of Genesis, God is presented as an ambitious and deeply interested Creator. God is determined to bring order and harmony from chaos and confusion, and to create an idyllic environment in which his creatures will dwell. The crown jewel of God's energetic efforts is our own creation in God's *image and likeness.* Just as the stage for its realization is being set, humankind shatters this dream. And ever since, a battle royal has ensued between God's all-encompassing, merciful love and the tenacious forces of sin and evil. To this day we have continued the shattering of God's dream in our own lives. But God refuses to allow this dream, conceived in divine love from all eternity, to be destroyed by the malice and sin in our hearts. Shattered, yes, but destroyed, never!

God's hope for us springs eternal! God continues to believe that ultimately we will succumb to the power and magnetism of the divine love and mercy. If God will never renege on the dream and the promises following from it, there is no reason for us to *ever* give up on ourselves, especially when we are in the stranglehold of our sins and rebellious tendencies.

While God established several covenants with the Israelites—who were represented by able leaders in the Hebrew Scriptures such as Noah, Abraham, Moses, David, and others—these covenants always left something to be desired. Humankind was never able to hold up our end of the commitment the way God did. After repeated failed attempts at restoration of the dream, the Lord came up with an extraordinary way of fulfilling it: God established a new and perfect covenant with us through Jesus. Jesus became one of us, joined to our humanity, and in this way bridged the chasm between God and humankind.

The second chapter explores the depth of God's commitment to this plan of salvation in Jesus Christ, while the third chapter focuses on the role of the Holy Spirit in God's plan of salvation. The Holy Spirit continues the work begun by God the Father since the beginning of time and brought to perfection in Jesus Christ. From the very beginning the plan belonged to the Triune God. Our awareness of the work of the Trinity has come to us principally through the life, death, and resurrection of Jesus. Yet the plan does not stop there. By God's grace, the reign of the Holy Spirit is the era of the Church. And it is in the service of the Church—which is God's community of believers—

that our discipleship grows and matures. The Holy Spirit is always abundantly present to be our advocate and guide.

Chapter Four focuses on the amazing truth that the Trinity has called each of us to participate in this divine plan of salvation. This call is not just made in general terms as a blanket invitation to whomever; it is a call made personally to each of us, *to you and to me.* Each of us is invited to become "holy, blameless in his sight and full of love" as only God is (Eph 1:4). This personal calling is central to the disciple's personal and intimate relationship with Jesus. Discipleship hinges on *union with the Master* and *walking continually in the Master's footsteps.*

Chapter Five focuses on the disciple's prayer. Prayer has become a necessity, a place of intimacy and renewal, a time of rest and formation. The disciple sits at the feet of the Master, and the Holy Spirit instructs and prepares the follower for the journey.

That formation process is carried over into the sixth and final chapter, in which the lifestyle of the disciple is examined. The worldview, attitudes, values, and everyday living of the disciple are looked at as a way of enhancing our own discipleship. Such a Christ-centered life is directed by the power of the Holy Spirit and maintained by the seeker's genuine desire to draw humbly closer to God.

"I am sure of this much: that he who has begun the good work in you will carry it to completion, right up to the day of Christ Jesus. It is my wish that you may be found rich in the harvest of justice which Christ Jesus has ripened in you, to the glory and praise of God" (Phil 1:6, 11).

My prayers and best wishes are with you!

CHAPTER ONE

God's Dream—
Faithful to the End

FASHIONING THE DREAM

The Book of Genesis is pivotal to understanding the Bible. In the first chapters the author sets the stage to capture vividly the depths of God's yearnings for us. God's decision, made before the dawning of space and time and surpassing all human understanding, is to offer the human inhabitants of a new universe, soon to be established, the privilege of participating in the divine life and heritage.

The creation of the universe is presented in graphic and compelling detail. The enthralling saga of God's creative genius unfolds verse by verse. Order and harmony emerge from chaos and confusion as God establishes what will be a familiar trademark of the divine Presence. God always brings order and harmony out of confusion and turmoil.

As the story progresses, there is an inexorable movement toward a finale. Powerful transformations emerge in quick succession: light is separated from darkness, day from night, heaven from earth, land from sea. The right circumstances have been created for the earth to bring forth vegetation. The creation of the heavenly bodies follows: the stars to separate day from night, the sun to govern the day, and the moon to govern the night. The water-creatures, birds, and animals are next to inhabit the earth.

Then with a master's stroke, God creates us, the crowning jewel of the Creator's handiwork.

> God created man in his image; in the divine image he created him; male and female he created them. God blessed them, saying: "Be fertile and multiply; fill the earth and subdue it. Have dominion over the fish of the sea, the birds of the air, and all the living things that move on the earth" (Gn 1:27–28).

Already we are learning what it means to be created in God's image and likeness. We have been given dominion over God's creatures, asked to exercise authority over them as God would. Furthermore, in the second account of creation, we are asked to name the animals and other creatures, another function that by right belongs only to God. Indeed, naming someone in Scripture is the equivalent of owning that person.

THE SPLINTERED DREAM

The final step in this act of majestic transformation is God's offer to Adam and Eve of the divine life *as a gift*, to be received freely and participated in wholeheartedly. God asks them to follow the divine dictates and not to wander off into their own willfulness. Yet they can choose to go against this life-enhancing choice toward God. Adam and Eve choose to succumb to temptation and disregard God's instructions. Their willfulness and pride hold sway. This story of rejecting God follows a pattern familiar in our own lives.

As a result of Adam and Eve's choice, evil entered the world and the inclination toward sin took root in our hearts. We always have to choose between good and evil. We are never able to have both God and evil at the same time. Choosing evil will always be choosing against God. So evil will always bring with it a trail of destruction, resulting from the rejection of God. Yet God's response to the sin of Adam and Eve is true to divine form.

THE PROMISE OF RESTORATION

The divine reaction is that God absolutely refuses to have the dream destroyed. God does not give up on Adam and Eve and their descendants. In keeping with this resolve, God makes a promise. "I will put enmity between you and the woman, and between your offspring and hers; He will strike at your head, while you strike at his heel" (Gn 3:15). The Church has understood these words to signify the promise of Jesus who would become man, take up our burden of sin, be our Savior and Lord, and bring to fulfillment God's plan for our salvation and restoration. At the same time, there will always be the struggle with sin in our lives and history.

The rest of the Old Testament demonstrates God's passionate commitment to Israel, making her the chosen people, in spite of her repeated infidelities and defiance. God never wavers in bringing this dream to fruition even though the forces of evil seem to have the upper hand at every turn. Every book in the Old Testament offers testimony to the wickedness of God's people, as well as to God's marvelous ability to demonstrate fidelity and covenantal love, to forgive and bring back, to offer hope and eventual restoration. In the process many heed the call to re-formation and re-creation. With God's help and power, individuals are transformed and God's dream is realized in their lives.

Let us look at a few examples of transformation and failure from the pages of the Hebrew Scriptures.

Moses: from Apprehensive to Assertive

In selecting Moses to bring the Israelites out of slavery and into the Promised Land, God makes it clear that liberation is *the work of divine hands.* Moses is the son of a Hebrew slave woman in Egypt. His origins are insignificant. He is found in the marshes where his mother had hidden him from her Egyptian masters, and is adopted by Pharaoh's daughter. As a young adult he flees Egypt after slaying an Egyptian who was mistreating one of his enslaved kinsmen.

One day, as Moses tends his sheep, God appears to him in a burning bush. He is told to go to Pharaoh as God's messenger to tell Pharaoh to let the enslaved Hebrew people go into the desert to worship their God. Moses is filled with dread and anxiety. He makes several attempts to refuse the summons, but God is persistent and very confident that their partnership will work. Hesitant but relenting, Moses ventures forth into Egypt to confront Pharaoh's might and obduracy.

Clearly, Moses is no match for this impossible mission, except that he knows that God is the real architect of the people's liberation. His role is to be a malleable instrument as God engages in another incredible transformation. The Exodus story has a sweep similar to the Creation story, a compelling backdrop of order and harmony coming out of chaos and confusion, and the mesmerizing revolution from bondage, ignominy, and chaos, to liberation, security, and community.

After crossing the Red Sea, it is tempting to think that the Israelites would put the worst of their trials and tribulations behind them. Yet now it is *their* stubbornness and wickedness that Moses has to confront. His commitment to his people, and God's faith in them, are severely tested. In the midst of their fickle murmurings and idolatry, God's everlasting love, constancy, and faithfulness to the Israelites shine forth. As God's faithful messenger, Moses is subjected to much suffering. Gradually, through many trials and tribulations, his leadership and holiness are acknowledged. He is recognized as the Law Giver and intermediary with God. In his later years he is recognized as God's beloved. His countenance is radiant with God's holiness. He successfully leads his people to the Promised Land, though he is not allowed to enter (Nm 20:6–13).

Several important truths about God's relationship to us emerge through this story. God is irrevocably committed to our salvation. It is God's passionate desire that we enter into communion with our Creator and become "holy and blameless in his sight, to be full of love" (Eph 1:4). And God will go to *any lengths* to realize this dream, provided we are willing and cooperative. The other sobering fact, *not of God's making*, is that we are capable of thwarting God's noble designs on our behalf, engaging in evil and thus bringing about our own destruction.

While the Hebrew people engage in idolatry and betrayal, much to the Creator's disappointment and frustration, God remains solicitous and deeply concerned about this stiff-necked people. In spite of their callousness, they gradually learn to accept God's place in their lives and history. They receive God's commandments and laws and make them the guiding principles of their lives, as well as their social order. They become a nation with God as their ruler. They worship the one, true God and enter into a covenant relationship with their Maker.

King David: from Man to Monarch

The genesis of the kings and kingdoms in Israelite history begins with a gradual falling away from God's designs. God's people want to be like the other nations around them who have kings as their rulers. God's kingship is no longer deemed enough. In no uncertain terms they choose to forget their origins and glorious history with God. They approach Samuel, the last just judge of Israel, and ask him to give them a king:

Samuel was displeased when they asked for a king to judge them. He prayed to the Lord, however, who said in answer: "Grant the people's every request. It is not you they reject, they are rejecting me as their king. As they have treated me constantly from the day I brought them up from Egypt to this day, deserting me and worshipping strange gods, so do they treat you too. Now grant their request; but at the same time, warn them solemnly and inform them of the rights of the king who will rule them" (1 Sm 8:6–9).

David is raised up as God's anointed one and becomes the foremost King of Israel. His reign as the second King of Israel is successful for many years because David is faithful to God's law. Israel flourishes and is considered a powerful nation. Then David moves away from God's purposes. He commits adultery with Bathsheba and has her husband murdered in battle. Eventually Nathan, his prophet, confronts him. David realizes his sin and asks God for forgiveness and mercy (Ps 51). From that moment he lives with a contrite and humbled heart, but he has to bear the consequences of his sin and waywardness.

There is turmoil in the kingdom and Absalom, his favorite son, rebels against David. They are at war with each other. David issues an order to his officers to make sure that his son's life is spared, if he is captured, as he wants reconciliation with him. Absalom is pursued by Joab, David's commander-in-chief, who slays him with three spikes driven into his heart when he finds him hanging by his long tresses from a terebinth tree (2 Sm 18:9–14). David's sorrow is overwhelming at the loss of his favorite son. In his old age, there is much turmoil in the kingdom and he accepts humiliation and scorn with a contrite heart as recompense for his wrongdoing.

Throughout his life God works with David, supporting him and providing solutions to apparently impossible situations. As long as David remains faithful to God's inspirations, he does well and is eminently successful. When his reign is blighted by scandal and tribulation, it is because he chose his own ways over God's commands. Through it all God remains faithful to David and his people, offering him mercy and forgiveness when he sins and acknowledges his guilt.

King Solomon: from Monarch to Mortal

In his old age, David decides to have his son, Solomon, crowned king after him. At first Solomon is a very wise king. Early in his reign he makes that wonderful prayer asking God for the gift of wisdom:

> The Lord was pleased that Solomon made this request. So God said to him: "Because you have asked for this—not for a long life for yourself, nor for riches, nor for the life of your enemies, but for understanding so that you may know what is right— I do as you requested. I give you a heart so wise and understanding that there has never been anyone like you up to now, and after you there will come no one to equal you. In addition, I give you what you have not asked for, such riches and glory that among kings there is not your like. And if you follow me by keeping my statutes and commandments, as your father David did, I will give you a long life" (1 Kgs 3:10–14).

His wisdom is legendary, as witnessed in his judgment about who is the rightful mother of the surviving child. The Queen of Sheba and other important luminaries come to seek Solomon's advice and wisdom. He is a very powerful king, much admired and respected by kingdoms near and far.

Perhaps his greatest contribution is completing the monumental task of building God's temple. Only then does he build his own palace. He is a very effective partner with God during the early years of his reign when he remains faithful to God's teaching and law.

In his later years, however, Solomon forsakes the true God of his ancestors and worships the gods of Baal. By forsaking the one, true God and the path of truth and justice, Solomon brings evil upon himself and his people. In the end, this *lack* of God-given wisdom leaves Solomon vulnerable to sin and corruption. This will be his royal legacy.

After Solomon's demise, corruption is rampant and wickedness flourishes among his successors. In fact, the kingdom is split between Israel and Judah because evil and malice are commonplace and God is forsaken. Even in such dire straits, God yearns for the salvation and reunion of the people. God holds on to the dream.

The Prophets: from Messengers of Misery to Heralds of Hope

Throughout the history of the kingdoms, God sends prophets to the kings and the people to bring them back to their Creator's path of truth and justice. The prophet's role is to speak boldly for God, challenging the people and their leaders with God's commands and promises. True prophets are not popular because of this confrontational stance. Yet they proclaim God's truth unequivocally, even though their message is often rejected. They preach that the destruction and exile of God's people is the consequence of their commitment to evil and idolatry. At the same time, they preach a message of mercy and salvation. It is in these messages that we get an insider's look into God's heart and the great passion God has for the people.

Isaiah

Isaiah is generally considered to be the greatest prophet. He is well liked in the beginning of his mission. But he soon becomes unpopular because his messages are so difficult to accept. He calls the people to repentance and warns them of God's judgment. The initial thirty-nine Chapters of the Book of Isaiah contain scathing denunciations as Isaiah calls Judah, Israel, and the surrounding nations to repent of their sins. However, the last twenty-seven Chapters are filled with consolation and hope as Isaiah unfolds God's promise of future blessings through the Messiah. Chapter 49 typifies God's covenantal commitment to the people:

> But Zion said, "The Lord has forsaken me; my Lord has forgotten me." Can a mother forget her infant, be without tenderness for the child of her womb? Even should she forget, I will never forget you. See, upon the palms of my hands I have written your name (Is 49:14–16).

Jeremiah

By the standards of the world, Jeremiah is a miserable failure. For forty years he serves as God's spokesperson to Judah. Consistently and passionately he urges the people to act, but nobody bothers to listen to him. He undergoes severe deprivations to deliver his prophecies. He is thrown into prison, and into a cistern, and is taken to Egypt against his will. Everyone—from family and friends to citizens and kings—reject him. Throughout his life, Jeremiah stands alone, declaring God's messages of doom, announcing the new covenant, and weeping over the fate of his beloved country. He does not marry as a sign that the destruction of God's people is at hand if they do not repent. When the people reject his warnings, Jeremiah moves to predicting specifically the destruction of Jerusalem and the events subsequent to its fall. The basic theme of his message is simple: "Return to God or your sins will devour you."

In the midst of this intensely sad chapter in the history of God's people, Jeremiah makes a very consoling prophecy. In Chapter 31, we read of the new covenant God will establish with the people:

> The days are coming, says the Lord, when I will make a new covenant with the house of Israel and the house of Judah. It will not be like the covenant I made with their fathers the day I took them by the hand to lead them forth from the land of Egypt; for they broke my covenant, and I had to show myself their master, says the Lord. But this is the covenant which I will make with the house of Israel after those days, says the Lord. I will place my law within them, and write it upon their hearts; I will be their God and they shall be my people. No longer will they have need to teach their friends and kinsmen how to know the Lord. All, from least to greatest, shall know me, says the Lord, for I will forgive their evil doing and remember their sin no more (Jer 31:31–34).

Hosea

Hosea is the first of the Minor Prophets. As predicted, Gomer, Hosea's wife, leaves him to pursue her lusts. But

Hosea, whose name means "salvation," finds her, redeems her, and brings her home again, fully reconciled.

Images of God's love, judgment, grace, and mercy toward the people are woven into Hosea's story. The love of God for Israel is like that of a husband for an unfaithful wife, great enough to forgive her infidelity if she will return to him, and ready to return to the beginning of their love that they may start anew. A covenant was made and God is faithful. God's love is steadfast. But Israel, like Gomer, is adulterous, spurning God's love and turning instead to false gods. Then, after warning of judgment, God reaffirms his love and offers reconciliation. His love and mercy are overflowing but justice will be served. Hosea seems to represent Yahweh as finally permitting the destruction of Israel. The historical Israel must perish, and there is no future for her except in a return to the desert, a new beginning. With God, the dream lives on.

CONCLUDING REMARKS

This chapter attempts a very sketchy reflection on the salient features of Israel's salvation history, beginning with the creation of the world and humankind. With the entrance of sin, God's wonderful dream of getting humans to share in the divine life is shattered. In tracing some significant periods of Israel's history, like the Exodus, the reigns of David and Solomon, and the activities of three prophets, we get an insider's view of God's intentions on our behalf. Israel is called to be the chosen people of God. God desires their sanctification as a nation. Leaders from among the people are selected to reveal and interpret God's designs for them, to act as God's intermediaries and spokespersons, to offer sacrifices of atonement and adoration. Some of these individuals like Abraham, Moses, and David are able to fathom the depths of God's intimacy and love for them and the people. The prophets, like Isaiah, Jeremiah, and Hosea among others, are also persons of great stature and spiritual depth as they attempt to be faithful to their calling of speaking boldly and truthfully in God's name.

This call to salvation is offered continually, in spite of Israel's unfaithfulness and idolatry. God never gives up on the people. God is an active participant in their affairs and history. They are always being beckoned forth to turn away from their sin and return in reconciliation to the Lord. This call has gone forth through the centuries and its echoes have reverberated in our hearts as well. We sense God's deliverance in the transformation of Moses. We learn from the lessons of the Old Testament that even great kings must live by the higher laws of God. We too have heard the soft and persistent voice of the Spirit of the prophets inviting us to come home to the Father, our first and only true love.

Exercise One
THE WORK OF THY FINGERS

▲ Scripture

The heavens declare the glory of God,
   and the firmament proclaims his handiwork.
Day pours out the word to day,
   and night to night imparts knowledge.
            —Psalm 19:1–2

▲ Summary

The creation of the world is a story about God. God's hand-iwork stirs wonder and reverence in our hearts, bringing up the inevitable question: Since Nature is so awe-inspiring, who must the Creator be? Our capacity to know and under-stand God being significantly limited, the divine Being will always be a mystery to us. While we might never be able to fully comprehend God's mystery, we can still be profoundly moved and transformed by it. It does much good to our spirits to be bathed and saturated in the beauty and grandeur around us. In this way the mystery comes to have significance for our lives and we are made aware that God is Emmanuel ("God with us").

▲ Session

(20–30 minute duration)

Take a few minutes to prepare yourself through the aware-ness of sounds in God's creation. Prostrate yourself, physi-cally or metaphorically, adoring your Maker and Lord. Then ask the Holy Spirit for the gift of understanding and grati-tude as you embark on the wondrous task of admiring God's masterpiece.

In *receptive silence* bring up images of God's creativity that have inspired and intrigued you, and allow the grandeur and mystery to wash over you: being saturated by the shim-mering sea, the placidity of the pond, the sacred silence of a sunset-emblazoned sky, the magnificence of the mountain range, the serenade of the songbird, the refinement of the rose, the dignity of the dandelion, and on and on.

In *loving silence* ponder the amazement of your own being and the gifts of smell, taste, sight, hearing, and touch. How intricately and superbly they serve us! How is our experience affected in their absence? Ponder your other faculties as well: imagination, memory, intellect, and free will. How admirably they serve us and how easily we take them for granted.

In *wondrous silence* ponder the joy within the laughter of a child; the unstinting devotion of your pet dog; the interplay of sunlight and shade in a forest glade; a lone eagle wafting on invisible air currents in a dappled sky; and on and on.

Finally, spend time with the Holy Trinity in thanksgiving, praise, and adoration resulting from your experience with God's creativity. The insights of self that you carry away from your encounter are God's gift to you.

▲ Reflection

Creation is a treasure trove of rich significance. For some it is the finger pointing skyward to the moon, indicating a reality that is very present in what we behold, yet is unfathomable. Our faith has pondered such reality and knows it to be God. God is love, and as John the Apostle tells us, God loved us *first*! Creation is an explicit sign of God's love for us. In receiving this love, a disciple responds in gratitude and engages in generous deeds that reflect the gift. It behooves us to spend much time contemplating the holy presence of God in the creatures around us and in our own being. Such pondering leads to a deep gratitude and generosity, which, hopefully, will lead to loving deeds.

Exercise Two
WONDERFULLY MADE

▲ Scripture

Then God said: "Let us make man in our image, after our likeness." . . . God created man in his image;
in the divine image he created him;
male and female he created them.
—Genesis 1:26–27

God chose us in him before the world began, to be holy and blameless in his sight, to be full of love; he likewise predestined us through Christ Jesus to be his adopted sons.
—Ephesians 1:4–6

▲ Summary

Who am I? This is a crucial question, and how we answer it on a continuing basis will determine the health of our spirituality. Over our lifetime, different answers from various sources have been proposed to us. At some point we decided to accept some of these conclusions as our own. Most assuredly, God too has addressed this question about our identity, telling us that we have been created in the divine image and likeness. We have been adopted as sons and daughters into the heavenly family through Jesus Christ. Have you taken the time to relish God's vision for you? Have you come to see God's determinations about who you are and accepted that revelation wholeheartedly as your own?

▲ Session

(20–30 minute duration)

Take some time to prepare yourself for this visit with God about your true identity, by reminding yourself that you are entering into the presence of your Creator and God who loves you passionately and has destined the divine family as your heritage.

Imagine yourself with God in beautiful surroundings, real or imagined. In a spirit of humble gratitude and reverence, you reflect *with God* about the following dimensions of your identity:

♦ You are God's own image and likeness. In spite of your limitations and brokenness, you have been "fearfully, wonderfully made" (Ps 139:14), "little less than the angels, and crowned . . . with glory and honor" (Psalm 8:6).

♦ You have been asked to take God's place in your dominion over creatures, to make sure that the earth is treated with appreciation and reverence, reflecting the same passion and benevolence that God revealed in creating it.

♦ You are God's adopted child, sharing in all the rights and privileges of the heavenly family already here on earth! You no longer possess the identity of outcast and slave that you had before your adoption.

♦ You have been called to be holy like God, which is another way of saying that you have been called to become totally other than who you ever could imagine you are.

♦ You have been called to be blameless in God's sight. This would remain a pipe dream were it not for God's passionate desire to transform us.

♦ You have been called to be full of love. Another pipe dream were it not God's passionate dream for you. God's ardent desire is that you become the image of God—full of love.

▲ Reflection

Psychology tells us who we are based on family traits and personal history. While religion and spirituality are not eliminated from the identity equation, generally they are not given much recognition. Ironically, many who have engaged in psychotherapy desire deeper answers to their questions, and invariably move toward spiritual sources. Meditating on God's truth about who we are can bring about a deep stillness and authenticity. Such serenity leads to a gentler acceptance of life's circumstances, deepening our trust that God works out everything for our good.

Exercise Three
THE MALICE OF SIN

▲ Scripture

The woman answered the serpent: "We may eat of the fruit of the trees in the garden; it is only about the fruit of the tree in the middle of the garden that God said, 'You shall not eat it or even touch it, lest you die.'" But the serpent said to the woman: "You certainly will not die! No, God knows well that the moment you eat of it your eyes will be opened and you will be like gods who know what is good and what is bad."

The woman saw that the tree was good for food, pleasing to the eyes, and desirable for gaining wisdom. So she took some of its fruit and ate it; and she also gave some to her husband, who was with her, and he ate it. Then the eyes of both of them were opened, and they realized that they were naked; so they sewed fig leaves together and made loin-cloths for themselves.

—Genesis 3:2–7

▲ Summary

Of its very nature sin creates illusion out of reality, cloaking itself under the guise of good, and making itself appealing and seductive. The serpent convinces Eve that God is a liar. Not only will she not die, he says, she will be like a god who knows what is truly good and bad. Before long the deception is revealed as Adam and Eve become aware that they are naked. As a consequence of their sin, their spirits are flawed and they become ashamed of who they are.

▲ Session

(20–30 minute duration)

Begin your prayer by asking the Holy Spirit to give you a receptive heart to truly understand the seductive malice of sin and your own strong tendency to allow its presence.

To help you receive a true understanding of sin, you can consider the following points in dialogue with God. Try to recognize similar traits in your own heart:

♦ In Adam and Eve's temptation, the serpent appeared convincing, reassuring, beguiling, and opposed to God's designs. He made God out to be a liar.

♦ In the story of Cain and Abel, some characteristics of sin are revealed: Cain is resentful of Abel because Abel is good; he kills his brother and lies about it, and he protests that the punishment for his heinous crime is too great. These characteristics point to sin as being self-serving.

♦ In the story of the golden calf, Aaron, who should have known better, makes an excuse to Moses, "You know well how prone the people are to evil" (Ex 32:23), and he went right ahead and abetted their desire to replace their God with a golden calf.

♦ David allows his lust for Bathsheba, a total stranger, to have the upper hand. He throws his covenant with God to the winds, commits adultery with her, has her husband killed in battle, and then marries her. Even an upright man like David was capable of sinning grievously against God.

▲ Reflection

Sin is devious and destructive, bearing all the hallmarks of the "Father of lies." The insidious aspect of sin is that it creates illusion out of reality, making evil seem good and attractive, and good appear blameworthy and wrong. Perhaps the greatest web of delusion that evil spins is for us to believe that we are better than we truly are, that we hardly commit sin, and/or that our sins do not have consequences.

Exercise Four
AN AUTHENTIC REPENTANCE

▲ Scripture

Then the LORD God said to the serpent: ". . . I will put enmity between you and the woman, and between your offspring and hers; He will strike at your head, while you strike at his heel."
—Genesis 3:14–15

Thus it was that John the Baptizer appeared in the desert, proclaiming a baptism of repentance which led to the forgiveness of sins.
—Mark 1:4

▲ Summary

As banished progeny of Eve, each of our lives is a tale of frustrated imaginings and failed resolutions. Still, hope springs eternal in this gloomy situation. The rainbow splashed across this shadowy horizon is God's promise of providing salvation to the sin-laden sojourner. The promise will never materialize without a radical turning toward God. While our earthly lives will always be filled with challenge, with God's help and our cooperation they will produce fruit worthy of God's reign among us.

▲ Session

(20–30 minute duration)

Take some time to prepare for this visit by asking the Holy Spirit for the gift of repentance.

When considering our sinfulness, there are two questions we need to address: Can I acknowledge my sins and the harm I have caused without excuses and alibis? Do I believe that God can and will forgive my sins if I am repentant? In this visit let us seek to address these questions with God. At some point in your dialogue, you might want to repeat some of the statements made by the following biblical figures:

- David was a sinner who was truly repentant. He believed that God would indeed forgive him his sins:

  > Have mercy on me, O God, in your
  >   goodness;
  >   in the greatness of your compassion
  >   wipe out my offense.
  > Thoroughly wash me from my guilt
  >   and of my sin cleanse me.
  > For I acknowledge my offense,
  >   and my sin is before me always (Ps 51:3–5).

- Jonah was sent to preach a message of doom to Nineveh, the traditional enemy of Israel. To his surprise, everyone from the king to the lowliest subject humbled themselves in sackcloth and ashes. Acknowledging their repentance, God did not carry out the punishment planned for them (see Jonah 3:4–10).

- The repentant criminal is a beautiful example of admission of sin and turning toward God:

  > But the other [criminal] rebuked him: "Have you no fear of God, seeing you are under the same sentence? We deserve it, after all. We are only paying the price for what we've done, but this man has done nothing wrong." He then said, "Jesus, remember me when you enter upon your reign." And Jesus replied, "I assure you: this day you will be with me in paradise" (Luke 23:40–43).

▲ Reflection

An authentic spiritual life delicately balances God's mercy towards us and our repentance towards God. When trying to understand mercy, it is easy to make God an ineffectual idol by watering down our need to make amends, and thus forget that this God is also holy and just. God's mercy can only be experienced as a divine characteristic when there is true repentance. Acknowledging our sins as they are, without excuse and hypocrisy, and making a commitment to live according to God's law in our hearts, brings about a true experience of God's mercy, which leads to repentance and action to make this world a better place.

Exercise Five
FAITH MADE
IMPREGNABLE BY FAITHFULNESS

▲ Scripture

Now Abraham and Sarah were old, advanced in years, and Sarah had stopped having her womanly periods. So Sarah laughed to herself and said, "Now that I am so withered and my husband is so old, am I still to have sexual pleasure?" But the LORD said to Abraham: "Why did Sarah laugh and say, 'Shall I really bear a child, old as I am?' Is anything too marvelous for the LORD to do? At the appointed time, about this time next year, I will return to you, and Sarah will have a son."

—Genesis 18:11–14

▲ Summary

In rebuking Thomas, Jesus made clear what faith is (see Jn 20:24-29). It is to believe when one does not see. In other words, faith is to believe when one does not perceive through, and rely on, merely human senses and understanding. Abraham had this faith that Jesus described. He believed that God would be true to the promise of giving him countless descendants, even though he was an elderly man. God remained faithful and, through the experience, purified and strengthened Abraham's faith to the point where, even had God chosen to take his son Isaac from him, he still would have believed that God could raise the child from the dead (Heb 11:19). God's faithfulness to us will never waver, and it is for us to adapt our faith to God's faithfulness.

▲ Session

(20–30 minute duration)

As you prepare for your visit with the God of Abraham, call to mind that this same God has made promises to you as well. Think about some of them as you enter into God's presence.

Visit with Abraham and Sarah in their tent. They recall their anxiety and trust when God asked them to leave Haran and settle in Canaan. Yet excitement bubbles up as they describe the amazing promise God made to them: their descendants will be abundant.

They talk about twenty-five years of waiting and wondering, in patience and doubt, for this wonderful promise. Abraham speaks about laughing when God appeared to him at the age of one hundred years to reiterate the promise. He wondered whether a child could be born to him at that age. Besides, Sarah was ninety. Sarah talks about laughing in disbelief as God's messengers spoke to Abraham in the tent and told him that within a year they would have a son.

There are tears in their eyes as they recount the marvelous event of their sunset years: the birth of Isaac, the realization of God's faithfulness! And with a distant look in his eyes, Abraham talks about how God tested him and told him to sacrifice Isaac. He was willing to do whatever God asked of him and Isaac was spared.

The moral of their story: put all your faith in God's faithfulness, even when God seems to have forgotten you.

Spend time with the God of Abraham, sharing the sentiments and reflections garnered from your visit with Abraham and Sarah as they apply to your own life.

▲ Reflection

When the chips are down, it is our faith that sustains and gives us purpose. The Christian grounds his or her faith on the knowledge that God has been and always will be faithful to the promises made. Sometimes it is the faith of others we know in the community of believers that will sustain our own faith. Such a bedrock conviction helps the disciple be patient and long-suffering in times of crisis and tribulation.

Exercise Six
THE CALL OF MOSES

▲ Scripture

But the LORD said, "I have witnessed the affliction of my people in Egypt and have heard their cry of complaint against their slave drivers, so I know well what they are suffering. Therefore I have come down to rescue them from the hands of the Egyptians and lead them out of that land into a good and spacious land, a land flowing with milk and honey. . . . So indeed the cry of the Israelites has reached me, and I have truly noted that the Egyptians are oppressing them. Come, now! I will send you to Pharaoh to lead my people, the Israelites, out of Egypt."

—Exodus 3:7–10

▲ Summary

The life of Moses highlights God's intense desire to be our liberator and redeemer. When chosen to lead his people out of Egypt into the Promised Land, Moses is a fugitive. He is convinced that he does not possess the qualities of a true leader. Grudgingly he embarks on the mission that God has given him. Barring a few missteps, he remains steadfast in his commitment to God and the people. In the end his face is aglow with God's holiness.

▲ Session

(20–30 minute duration)

Prepare yourself for your visit by reciting a short aspiration: My God (in breath), my All (out breath). This was St. Francis of Assisi's prayer. When you are ready, visit with Moses over his discipleship:

♦ Moses talks about how he was found by Pharaoh's daughter. He reflects on his life in the palace and how he killed an Egyptian who was ill-treating a Hebrew.

- As a fugitive he encounters God at the burning bush. He speaks of the odd experience of being overwhelmed by God's holiness while simultaneously being reluctant to accept God's mission to Egypt.

- He tells of Pharaoh's cunning during the ten plagues. It was a time of divine manifestations and much dread and confusion. In spite of his own anxiety, Moses knew God was in charge.

- The wanderings in the desert are the main focus of his narration: the awesome ecstasy of meeting God and receiving the ten commandments, his shock and anger at the idolatry of the people, and promulgating God's laws.

- He speaks with amazement of his transformation from a fearful and diffident introvert to a recognized leader and Law Giver to his people.

- Finally, he talks about his special moments with God: God's appearance in the burning bush, his position as the people's leader and representative before God, his role as intercessor for his rebellious people, his lack of faith in God's power at Meribah, his graceful acceptance of God's decision that he could view the Promised Land but not enter it.

With reverence and gratitude, come before the God of Moses, and share your sentiments and reflections in prayerful dialogue. What then is God asking of you?

▲ Reflection

Wisdom is born of the understanding that God is supreme, and God's ways are the best. In this sense, a wise person is holy. The wise person is willing to stake everything—property, possessions, and even life—in order to be possessed by God. A wise person becomes God's presence in the community, and God's power is manifest in him or her. Moses, indeed, was such a person.

Exercise Seven
THE CALL OF SAMUEL

▲ Scripture

The next time her husband Elkanah was going up with the rest of his household to offer the customary sacrifice to the LORD and to fulfill his vows, Hannah did not go, explaining to her husband, "Once the child is weaned, I will take him to appear before the LORD and to remain there forever; I will offer him as a perpetual nazirite"
—1 Samuel 1:21–22

▲ Summary

Samuel is set apart for the Lord even before his conception. His mother, Hannah, makes a pact with God. She asks God for a child to end her reproach of barrenness. In turn she will set the child apart for the Lord's service. Her husband acquiesces to her vow and prays that the Lord will bring her resolve to fulfillment. Both Hannah and her son, Samuel, take their commitment to God very seriously. She is able to offer her son to God's service because of this steadfastness.

▲ Session

(20–30 minute duration)

Take a few minutes to prepare for your visit with God. Ask the Holy Spirit to teach you the lessons you need to learn from the faithful examples of Hannah and Samuel.

♦ In your visit with Hannah, you ponder the vow she made to God: "O LORD of hosts, if you look with pity on the misery of your handmaid, if you remember me and do not forget me, if you give your handmaid a male child, I will give him to the LORD for as long as he lives; neither wine nor liquor shall he drink, and no razor shall ever touch his head" (1 Sm 1:11).

♦ She tells of the Lord's favor upon her: "The LORD favored Hannah so that she conceived and gave birth to three more sons and two daughters, while young Samuel grew up in the service of the LORD" (1 Sm 2:21).

♦ In your visit with Samuel, you reflect on his call. His mother approached Eli and said: "Pardon, my lord! As you live, my lord, I am the woman who stood near you here, praying to the LORD. I prayed for this child, and the LORD granted my request. Now I, in turn, give him to the LORD; as long as he lives, he shall be dedicated to the LORD" (1 Sm 1:26–28). She left him there.

♦ You reflect with Samuel on his bittersweet experiences in God's service. As a prophet he told Eli of the destruction of his family. As Israel's greatest judge he led during some of their most troubled times. He was assigned by God to anoint Saul, and later David, as kings of Israel. He suffered greatly as his sons turned away from God, took bribes, and perverted justice.

Bring your sentiments to God and reflect on your own life and where God might be calling you.

▲ *Reflection*

Hannah and Samuel were persons of genuine integrity. Hannah was willing to set aside her own deep attachment to Samuel and dedicate him to God's service. She possessed an undivided heart. Like his mother, Samuel carried out his responsibilities to God faithfully and justly. He was widely acknowledged as a man who lived by God's law. He remained faithful to God even though his missions were often very difficult and dangerous, consuming much of his physical and emotional energy.

Exercise Eight
THE CALL OF JEREMIAH

▲ Scripture

The word of the LORD came to me thus: Before I formed you in the womb I knew you, before you were born I dedicated you, a prophet to the nations I appointed you.

—Jeremiah 1:4–5

▲ Summary

At great cost, Jeremiah accepts God's call to be a prophet. He was obedient to God's summons to preach a message of doom and repentance, and risks everything, even his own life. On many occasions he feels that God has let him down and even duped him. However, his faith always proves to be more steadfast than his discouragement and despair. Scorned and abandoned by his people, he is special in God's plan.

▲ Session

(20–30 minute duration)

Take some time asking the Holy Spirit to prepare you for this visit with God and to give you a deep acceptance of God's will in your life.

Visit with Jeremiah at the end of forty years of serving God faithfully, and ask him to enlighten you about faithfulness to God's will. He speaks to you in the first person. After every reflection, you take some time to absorb his sentiments:

♦ I was a mere youth when God called me. Before I knew it I was caught up in a whirlwind of controversy, strife, and threats to my life.

♦ I was asked by God not to marry as a sign to my people of their impending destruction.

- I experienced much loneliness and dread as I prophesied the seventy-year captivity in Babylon and my people's eventual return from exile.

- Before the fall of Jerusalem the king and his people rejected me and became my enemies. The officials threw me into a cistern to die, but Ebed-melech rescued me. After the fall I was exiled to Egypt. I was alienated even from my family and friends.

- My grief over my people's suffering was incurable. I was broken and disconsolate by the ruin of my people, and came to be known as the "weeping prophet."

- I always acted as God's faithful messenger in spite of many attempts on my life because I knew that God was calling the people to repentance.

Finally, spend some time with the God of Jeremiah and listen to the feedback God gives you about his faithful servant and son and what you can learn from the life of the prophet.

▲ Reflection

Jeremiah's life is both intriguing and inspiring. It raises difficult questions for our limited comprehension of God's love for us, and the necessity of good people having to suffer. At the same time, Jeremiah's life brings us face to face with God's mystery. We will always walk in darkness before this mystery. As long as faith illuminates the darkness of God's mystery, it makes sense to live with our questions and wait on God to give us the answers that we so desperately seek.

Exercise Nine
THE TRUE CONSOLATION

▲ Scripture

Comfort, give comfort to my people, says your God. Speak tenderly to Jerusalem, and proclaim to her that her service is at an end, her guilt is expiated; Indeed, she has received from the hand of the LORD double for all her sins.

—Isaiah 40:1–2

▲ Summary

Isaiah was a strong and courageous prophet. He had an active ministry for 60 years before he was executed during Manasseh's reign according to tradition. He called the people to turn from their lives of sin and warned them of God's judgment. Chapters 40–66 of Isaiah are filled with consolation and hope as Isaiah unfolds God's promise of future blessings through the Messiah.

▲ Session

(20–30 minute duration)

Spend a few minutes getting ready for your visit with God. He is about to unfold before you the dreams and promises of the divine heart.

Imagine you are in exile in Babylon and have just heard the decree by Cyrus to release the remnant captives and allow them to return to Jerusalem. You ponder on God's promises made to you through Isaiah as you prepare to return to Jerusalem. You do this by repeating over and over some of the key phrases contained in the promises:

♦ Fear not, for I have redeemed you; I have called you by name: you are mine. When you pass through the water, I will be with you; in the rivers you shall not drown. When you walk through fire, you shall not be burned; the flames shall not consume you. For I am the LORD your God, the Holy One of Israel, your savior (Is 43:1–3). *Words of great consolation for a captive just set free.*

♦ But Zion said, "The LORD has forsaken me; my Lord has forgotten me." Can a mother forget her infant, be without tenderness for the child of her womb? Even should she forget, I will never forget you. See, upon the palms of my hands I have written your name (Is 49:14–16). *God seems to project the self-image of a romantic, youthful lover who has your name etched in the palms of his hands.*

♦ Fear not, you shall not be put to shame; you need not blush, for you shall not be disgraced. The shame of your youth you shall forget, the reproach of your widowhood no longer remember. For he who has become your husband is your Maker; his name is the LORD of hosts; your redeemer is the Holy One of Israel, called God of all the earth (Is 54:4–5). *Words of great tenderness, compassion, and redemption.*

♦ Lo, I am about to create new heavens and a new earth; the things of the past shall not be remembered or come to mind. Instead, there shall always be rejoicing and happiness in what I create; for I create Jerusalem to be a joy and its people to be a delight. I will rejoice in Jerusalem and exult in my people (Is 65:17–19). *The heralding of a new era and a new and everlasting covenant.*

▲ *Reflection*

God's Word is living and true. Isaiah's prophecies sustain our faith and optimism in God's faithfulness to us. The truths contained in these prophecies are of timeless value. Each time we ponder on them, God's truth and presence are made alive in us.

Exercise Ten
THE NEW COVENANT

▲ *Scripture*

But this is the covenant which I will make with the house of Israel after those days, says the LORD. I will place my law within them, and write it upon their hearts; I will be their God, and they shall be my people. . . . All, from the least to greatest, shall know me, says the LORD, for I will forgive their evildoing and remember their sin no more.

—Jeremiah 31:33–34

▲ *Summary*

Jeremiah, the prophet, is prepared to preach a difficult message of confrontation and repentance because of the conviction that God loves us and wants to bring us salvation and freedom. Jeremiah's trust in God's faithfulness, amidst sin and betrayal, was made possible because he knew that God would never give up on the people and would establish a new and eternal covenant. Only such faith and hope can sustain a disciple's life and mission.

▲ *Session*

(20–30 minute duration)

Take a few minutes to come home to yourself through the awareness of sounds, or your breathing, or your bodily sensations.

Enter into a loving dialogue with God the Father regarding the prophecy made by Jeremiah about the new covenant:

♦ The old covenant, broken by the people, is replaced by a new covenant. This new covenant will never need to be replaced. *What does this say to you about God?*

♦ Paul tells us in Hebrews 8:6 that Christ is the mediator of a better covenant, founded on better promises.

Express your sentiments of gratitude and eagerness to respond in deeds of kindness and charity.

♦ This new covenant is revolutionary, involving not only Israel and Judah, but the Gentiles as well. It offers a unique personal relationship with God, with the divine laws written in our hearts instead of on stone. God pledges to forgive our evildoing and remember our sins no more. *Continue to express your sentiments of gratitude for God's goodness as well as sorrow for sins committed against God and your fellow humans.*

▲ *Reflection*

Ezekiel graphically expresses the new era that will be established with the new covenant given through Jeremiah:

> I will sprinkle clean water upon you to cleanse you from all your impurities, and from all your idols I will cleanse you. I will give you a new heart and place a new spirit within you, taking from your bodies your stony hearts and giving you natural hearts. I will put my spirit within you and make you live by my statutes, careful to observe my decrees. You shall live in the land I gave your fathers; you shall be my people and I will be your God (Ez 36:25–28).

CHAPTER GLEANINGS

▲ We will always have to choose between good and evil. We will never be able to have both God and evil at the same time. Choosing evil will always be choosing against God, so evil will always bring with it a trail of destruction resulting from our rejection of God.

▲ God is always beckoning us forth, calling us to turn away from our sins and return to the Lord. This call has gone forth through the centuries and its echoes have reverberated in our hearts. We hear a soft and persistent voice inviting us to come home to God, our first and only true love.

▲ It behooves us to spend much time contemplating the holy presence of God in the creatures around us and in our own being. Such pondering leads to a deep gratitude and generosity, which hopefully, will lead to loving deeds.

▲ Wisdom is born of the understanding that God is supreme and God's ways are the best. In this sense, a wise person is holy.

▲ When trying to understand mercy, it is easy to make God an ineffectual idol by watering down our need to make amends and thus forget that this God is also holy and just. God's mercy can only be experienced as a divine characteristic when there is true repentance.

▲ As long as faith illuminates the darkness of God's mystery, it makes sense to live with our questions and wait on God to give us the answers that we so desperately seek.

▲ The Christian grounds his or her faith on the knowledge that God has been and always will be faithful to the promises made. Such a bedrock conviction helps the disciple be patient and long-suffering in times of crisis and tribulation.

Faith is to believe when one does not see. It is our job to adapt our faith to God's faithfulness.

CHAPTER TWO

God's Dream—
Refreshed and Restored

THE MESSIANIC PROMISES

Several centuries before the advent of Jesus, the prophets spoke of his coming. The promise of God's Anointed One brought the Israelites unprecedented hope. These prophecies were made when Israel was in dire straits. The people had abandoned the ways of God and were sent into many years of exile. For hundreds of years the Israelites held on to the reassuring promise of the Messiah.

MICAH

Micah is fearless in his attacks on the establishment of his time, especially those who would take advantage of the poor and downtrodden. He challenges the corrupt priests and prophets, as well as the fraudulent merchants and unjust judges. Still, in the midst of these condemnations, he speaks of the restoration of Israel and the promise of the Messiah (Mi 4:14–5:1–5). Micah says that the next king in David's line will be the Messiah who will establish a kingdom that will never end. Mighty Jerusalem, with all its wealth and power, will be besieged and destroyed. Its king cannot save it. In contrast, Bethlehem, a tiny town, will be the birthplace of the only king who can save his people. The Messiah will be born in Bethlehem (Lk 2:4–7) and eventually reign as the eternal King (Rv 19–22).

ISAIAH

Isaiah's prophecies reveal the future Redeemer through four *Servant-of-the-Lord* oracles. In the first oracle, recorded at the beginning of Chapter 42, he is described as God's chosen one who is filled with God's spirit. He will bring forth justice to the nations through mercy and compassion. "A bruised reed he shall not break, and a smoldering wick he shall not quench, until he establishes justice on the earth" (Is 42:3–4).

In the second oracle, Chapter 49:1–7, Isaiah speaks of a redeemer designated by God from conception for a special station in life. He is a suffering servant whose vocation will be not only the restoration of Israel, but also the conversion of the world. "It is too little, he says, for you to be my servant, to raise up the tribes of Jacob, and restore the survivors of Israel; I will make you a light to the nations, that my salvation may reach to the ends of the earth" (Is 49:6).

In the third oracle, Chapter 50:4–11, the redeemer is portrayed as one who speaks words of consolation and inspiration to the weary. He does not refuse the divine vocation and as a result submits willingly to insults and beatings. "I gave my back to those who beat me, my cheeks to those who plucked my beard; my face I did not shield from buffets and spitting" (Is 50:6).

In the last oracle, Chapters 52:13–53:12, Isaiah gives us an extraordinary description of the sinless Servant, who by his voluntary suffering atones for the sins of his people and saves them from just punishment at the hands of God.

Only in Jesus Christ are these sweeping prophecies fulfilled. The idea of saving the world through a humble, suffering servant rather than a glorious king is contrary to human thought and worldly pride. Even religious Jews, like Peter and the disciples, assumed that Israel would receive a political Messiah, a king who would bring salvation in the form of deliverance from their enemies and colonizers. Yet the Messiah's strength would be shown in humility, suffering, and mercy.

JESUS—THE QUINTESSENTIAL PARABLE

In keeping with the prophecies, the life and teachings of Jesus portray him as the quintessential parable that shatters the parameters of human logic. Jesus draws conclusions that challenge our stereotypes about the nature and designs of God. At first glance these conclusions seem to be ludicrous and without much substance, but on closer scrutiny they clearly contain within them a revolution of salvation and peace.

The circumstances of Jesus' birth set the stage immediately. He was born in Bethlehem of a virgin named Mary. There was no reason for Mary to declare that her child was conceived by the power of the Holy Spirit. Such an assertion would have been both laughable and hypocritical to the average person, who would naturally conclude that she was covering up for her sin of adultery (betrothal had the same binding force as marriage). Mary's pregnancy was a dangerous liability, as it could only bring her shame, dishonor, and even death by stoning. Yet she trusted the Holy Spirit's action in her life; she was "the servant of the LORD" (Lk 1:38). Mary believed with all her heart that God's ways would prevail.

Similarly, Joseph would have no real advantage in keeping Mary as his wife after he found out that she was pregnant. There would be much difficult scrutiny to withstand. After intense soul-searching he made the decision "to divorce her quietly" (Mt 1:19). Then it was made clear to him in a dream that his betrothed's pregnancy was an act of God. He became Mary's husband and remained committed to God's design for her, regardless of the consequences.

The consequences were indeed many and difficult. Their child was born in a stable in Bethlehem, far from their homes and families in Nazareth. They were subjected to Herod's decision to slay all male children two years old and under, and had to flee to Egypt to protect the child, remaining there until Herod's death. At the presentation in the temple, they were left with no doubt that their child indeed belonged to God. In carrying out God's designs, he would pierce their hearts. The mounting opposition to Jesus during his public life and the excruciating circumstances of his crucifixion and death did, indeed, crush their spirits.

THE PARABLE AS A TEACHING TOOL

Jesus used the parable as a principal teaching tool. The parables give us deep insight into Jesus. For the pure of heart longing for the good news of salvation, the parables break new ground and lead to the saving presence of God. They are stumbling blocks for the self-reliant and resistant. Through the parables Jesus revealed God's total investment in us; his willingness to go to *any length* to be merciful and compassionate to the repentant sinner. They also emphasized the fact that God's thoughts surpass our understanding. Let us look at a sampling of his parables to know Jesus better.

The Pharisee and the Tax Collector

In Luke 18, Jesus tells us that a Pharisee prayed in the temple with unbowed head: "I give you thanks, O God, that I am not like the rest of men—grasping, crooked, adulterous—or even like this tax collector. I fast twice a week. I pay tithes on all I possess." The Pharisee's prayer is a boast and a demand. He believed he had merited salvation through his observances. As for the tax collector, we are told he "kept his distance, not even daring to raise his eyes to heaven. All he did was beat his breast and say, 'O God, be merciful to me, a sinner.'" Here was a man who was deeply aware of how he had offended God. In prostration he asked to be forgiven and saved.

Jesus passes judgment on both men. The tax collector went away justified, but the Pharisee did not. Jesus makes it clear that we can only be saved through a humble acknowledgment of our sins and sincere petitioning of God's forgiveness. Jesus came for the sinner. The repentant sinner always has a home in God's heart.

The Parables of Divine Mercy

Luke Fifteen is memorable because of the three parables about God's mercy. There is a common refrain at the end of the first two parables about the lost sheep and the lost silver coin. Jesus tells us that "there will likewise be more joy in heaven over one repentant sinner than over ninety-nine righteous people who have no need to repent" (Lk 15:7). If we believe this statement and base our lives on it, we will be transformed!

In the parable of the Prodigal Son we can empathize with the older son's attitude. He is disgusted that his father would celebrate his younger brother's return home after he had spent his entire inheritance on "loose women." The father's reply is profound in its simplicity: "But we had to celebrate and rejoice! This brother of yours was dead, and has come back to life. He was lost, and is found" (Lk 15:32). Great indeed is the power of God's compassion for the sinner! Returning to such a God is coming back to one's roots, which is indeed the only true and lasting homecoming.

MIRACLES—SIGNS OF GOD'S REIGN

Jesus worked many miracles, with one purpose in mind. Miracles were signs that the reign of God was present in our midst and Jesus was indeed the Promised One and the Son of God. As a result, miracles occurred in the context of faith. Both the healed and the onlookers were challenged to accept Jesus as the Messiah. The miracles always demanded faith and an acceptance of Jesus as the way to God. A closer look at two of Jesus' miracles reveals the pattern of faith leading to the miracle and then being strengthened by it.

The Paralyzed Man Cured

Luke's gospel describes the curing of a paralyzed man in Chapter 5:17–26. Jesus was teaching in the middle of a large crowd that included Pharisees and rabbis from Judea, Galilee, and Jerusalem. Some men were trying to bring a friend who was paralyzed to see Jesus, but they were unable to get his mat through the crowd, so they lowered him through the roof.

Jesus recognized their faith and forgave the man's sins, and then, to show the disbelieving Pharisees that he did have that power, he healed the man as well. "He picked up the mat he had been lying on and went home praising God" (Lk 5:25). The crowd also began to praise God. The miracle of healing, worked in response to the men's faith, calls forth an even greater expression of faith and praise from the men and from the crowd as well.

The Man Born Blind

In John's gospel, Chapter Nine is devoted to the story of the man who was born blind, and whom Jesus cures. The heart of the story is the increasing faith and witness of the blind man to Jesus' healing power and compassion.

The man's faith was great indeed; after being healed he became a person of courage and integrity. We are told that Jesus sought him out when he heard of his rejection by the unbelieving Pharisees. In their conversation Jesus invited the man to believe in the Son of Man who was now speaking to him. The man's spontaneous reply was, "I do believe, Lord." And he bowed down to worship Jesus. In that moment of adoration, the man who was healed by Jesus became his disciple. He learned to see that Jesus was far more than "that man they call Jesus"; he was the Messiah.

JESUS—THE SUFFERING SERVANT

Perhaps the most difficult aspect of Jesus' life and mission was his identification as suffering servant. The messianic prophecies tell us that Jesus bore our infirmities and endured our sufferings. "He was pierced for our offenses, crushed for our sins, upon him was the chastisement that makes us whole, by his stripes we were healed. We had all gone astray like sheep, each following his own way; but the LORD laid upon him the guilt of us all" (Is 53:5–6).

During his public ministry Jesus made reference to his impending passion and death repeatedly. In Matthew 16, Jesus indicated for the first time that he "must go to Jerusalem and suffer greatly there at the hands of the leaders, the chief priests, and the scribes, and to be put to death, and raised up on the third day" (Mt 16:21). Peter is unable to tolerate the news, as it is contrary to all his expectations of Israel being liberated by a political Messiah. It seems apparent at this point that Peter did not understand the prophecies and the full extent of Jesus' mission. Yet just a short time before, Peter was taking the stand that, "You are the Messiah, the Son of the Living God."

In Chapter Seventeen, Matthew describes the Transfiguration and then presents the healing of the possessed boy by Jesus, after the disciples failed in their attempt to heal him because they lacked faith. In this context of divine transcendence and power, Jesus makes the second prophecy of his death and resurrection. "The Son of Man is going to be delivered into the hands of men who will put him to death, and he will be raised up on the third day" (Mt 17:22–23). The disciples are grief-stricken. They are not able, as yet, to comprehend Jesus' resurrection on the third day. They are preoccupied with his impending death and the destruction of their messianic vision.

In Matthew's Twentieth chapter, Jesus reiterates the fulfillment of God's plan of salvation through him.

> "We are going up to Jerusalem now. There the Son of Man will be handed over to the chief priests and scribes, who will condemn him to death. They will turn him over to the Gentiles, to be made sport of and flogged and crucified. But on the third day he will be raised up" (Mt 20:18–19).

In a mysterious and paradoxical way, Jesus' hour of suffering and disgrace is also his hour of glorification.

> "The hour has come for the Son of Man to be glorified. I solemnly assure you, unless the grain of wheat falls to the earth and dies, it remains just a grain of wheat. But if it dies it produces much fruit. . . . My soul is troubled now, yet what should I say—Father, save me from this hour? But it was for this

that I came to this hour. Father, glorify your name!"
Then a voice came from the sky: "I have glorified it,
and will glorify it again" (Jn 12:23–24, 27–28).

JESUS—THE HEART OF THE PASSOVER

The identification of Jesus as suffering servant reaches
its climax in the Passover supper. The Passover meal com-
memorates the Exodus from slavery in Egypt, the great
saving event of Israel's history and its foundation as the
people of God. A year-old unblemished male lamb was
slaughtered for the meal and its blood was applied to the
doorposts and lintel of every house as a sign that no
destruction would come from the avenging angel.

The first Passover supper was celebrated in anticipa-
tion of the saving event that was to occur that night in
Egypt (see Ex 12). A meal likewise anticipates the new
Passover. Jesus is the new Passover Lamb and is consumed
sacramentally by the disciples, the small core of the New
Israel living according to a New Way.

The motif of atonement is explicit during the meal.
After Jesus offers his body as food, he takes a cup, gives
thanks, and gives it to them. "'All of you must drink from
it,' he said, 'for this is my blood, the blood of the covenant,
to be poured out in behalf of many for the forgiveness of
sins'" (Mt 26:26–28).

The sacrificial motif of the Passover is likewise explicit
in the conception of the Eucharist as a sacrificial banquet.
This is clearly stated by Paul (1 Cor 10:14–22), as the con-
sumption of the Eucharist is a decisive reason for the pro-
hibition of any participation in pagan sacrifices by
Christians. The new Passover is a memorial as well. Every
time the Eucharist is celebrated, the saving event is reenact-
ed and each participant experiences the event and is personally integrated into the death and resurrection of Jesus.

THE RISEN LORD—MIRACLE AND PARABLE

The resurrection event is the resounding confirmation
and fulfillment of the messianic prophecies. The resurrection
and the events leading to it make no sense to the rationalist
and unbeliever. To the believer, whose faith in Jesus has been
a source of transformation, the resurrection is the surest sign

of hope that the saving presence of God has come into our midst. The faithful recognize a sound logic within the testimonies of the witnesses.

After Jesus' death, his disciples were in disarray. They cowered in fear and worry about their lives. In Luke 24 we are told that the women in the group went at dawn on the first day of the week to embalm Jesus' body with spices. They had not been able to do this at the time of his burial because of Sabbath Day restrictions. On approaching the tomb they were mystified by the fact that the huge stone had been rolled away from the entrance. Who could have done it? When they entered the tomb they could not find Jesus' body.

While they were puzzling over this strange happening, two men in brilliant garments stood beside them. Understandably the women were terrified. They knew they were witnessing something very strange and mysterious as it was taking place. They bowed to the ground. The men said them: "Why do you search for the Living One among the dead? He is not here; he has been raised up. Remember what he said to you while he was still in Galilee . . ." (Lk 24:5–6).

When the women returned to the eleven remaining disciples and told them what they had seen the story seemed like nonsense, and the group refused to believe them. Their reaction suggests that the disciples did not anticipate Jesus' resurrection, much less have the idea of creating a resurrection myth by removing his body. Peter and John, however, got up and ran out to the tomb. Peter stooped down to look into the tomb and could see nothing but the empty wrappings. They too went away full of amazement, wondering what to believe.

There were other stories of discouragement and disbelief. On that same first day of the week, two disciples were making their way to Emmaus, discussing what had happened. Before long Jesus joined their company. However, they were restrained from recognizing him. In response to Jesus' queries about the latest events, they expressed their shattered hope in Jesus as Israel's Messiah. They also told Jesus about the women's experience at the tomb and the story conveyed by Peter and John.

In gradual increments Jesus opened their hearts and minds. He began by speaking about Moses and all the prophets and interpreted every passage of Scripture that referred to him. By now they were near the village of Emmaus. Upon their insistence, Jesus agreed to spend more time that night with them. During the meal, Jesus took bread, pronounced the blessing, broke the bread, and distributed it to them. Within the significance of that moment, their eyes were opened and they recognized him. Then Jesus vanished from their sight and they implored one another, "Were not our hearts burning inside us as he talked to us on the road and explained the Scriptures to us?" (Lk 24:32).

They returned immediately to Jerusalem, where they found the Eleven and the rest of the company together. They were greeted with, "The Lord has been raised! It is true! He has appeared to Simon" (Lk 24:34–35). With festive hearts they recounted what had happened and how they had known him "in the breaking of the bread."

Meanwhile, John tells us in Chapter Twenty that Jesus appeared to the disciples while secluded on the evening of that first day of the week. Thomas was absent when Jesus came. The other disciples witnessed to him: "We have seen the Lord!" His answer was simple; "I will never believe it without probing the nail prints in his hands, without putting my finger in the nail marks and my hand into his side."

A week later the disciples were once more in the room, and this time Thomas was with them. Despite the locked doors, Jesus came and stood before them. "Peace be with you," he said to all present. Then he fixed his attention on Thomas: "Take your finger and examine my hands. Put your hand into my side. Do not persist in your unbelief, but believe!"

Thomas said in response, "My Lord and my God!"

Jesus then said to him: "You became a believer because you saw me. Blest are they who have not seen and have believed" (see Jn 20:24–29).

CONCLUSION

There is perhaps no better way to sum up Jesus' life and teachings than by mulling over the fulfillment of God's plan of salvation through him as recorded by Paul in his letter to the Ephesians. "Praised be the God and Father of our Lord Jesus Christ, who has bestowed on us in Christ every spiritual blessing in the heavens!" (Eph 1:3). Those blessings, which we will enjoy in full abundance in heaven, are already ours here on earth! Paul goes on to say "God chose us in him before the world began, to be holy and blameless in his sight, to be full of love . . . to be his adopted [sons and daughters]" (Eph 1:4–5).

When Paul referred to us as God's adopted sons and daughters, he was speaking both as a Roman citizen and Jew. When an alien or slave became a Roman citizen, every privilege and right belonging to the Roman family was conferred on the adopted one. No longer did the new citizen have to worry about the vestiges of servitude.

As a Jew, Paul was deeply aware of Jewish sentiment over the adoption of a person into the family. In adopting a stranger, child or adult, the family made a conscious, life-long commitment to him or her, as they would to their own flesh and blood. Through Jesus Christ, God adopted us and made us integral members of the divine family, perfectly bridging the gap created by alienation and sin.

Even more startling is the fact that God is a blatant optimist when it comes to creating dreams in our regard. Paul tells us that God chose us "to be holy and blameless in his sight, to be full of love" (Eph 1:4). It seems rather astonishing, given the unfaithful history of God's people, that our Lord continually hopes and dreams that we will come to live in Christ's image. Yet such is the power of God's salvation through Jesus. This is the transformation that takes place in any individual who, like the blind man, accepts Jesus as Savior and Lord, and humbles his entire being in submission to Him as the Son of the Living God. God's dream for us is holiness, blamelessness, and genuine love.

God's plan of salvation in and through Jesus challenges conscious thought and ignites the imagination. God chose to unite us with the Triune God through Jesus becoming human. Jesus identified with us in all things, while defeating sin, and through him we have been guaranteed access into God's life and heart. We have been made God's very own sons and daughters, and it is our privilege and birthright to share in God's dream to live holy and blameless lives, full of love, as God is full of love. God's plan for us, envisaged from all eternity, and given the breath of life in our creation at the beginning of time, has now been brought to fulfillment and completion in Jesus Christ.

Exercise Eleven
BELIEVING IS SEEING

▲ Scripture

"If you were blind there would be no sin in that. 'But we see,' you say, and your sin remains."
—John 9:41

▲ Summary

Giving sight to a man born blind is the event. This miracle evokes belief in some and a closed and hardened heart in others. Some accept the sign from God. Others argue that Jesus could not have come from God because he broke the community's rules regarding the Sabbath. The Scribes and Pharisees recognize that Jesus is challenging their authority and threatening their security, so they falsify the signs he gave them and discredit him in any way they can. In the case of the blind man, he has received the gift of sight. He *knows* he is in the presence of the divine. In bowing down and worshiping Jesus as his Savior he comes to *see and understand* even more deeply. In the case of the community's leaders, their "sight" was dimmed. Their lack of faith was spiritual blindness. Believing is seeing.

▲ Session

(20–30 minute duration)
Take a few minutes to appreciate your gift of sight and the numerous blessings you have received through it. Imagine how it would feel to live in a world of darkness all your life. In humble gratitude ask the Holy Spirit to enhance your eyes of faith so that you might be able to *see and understand* even more deeply that Jesus is your Savior and Lord.

You can use the four steps of *lectio divina* to pray on this miracle: reading, repetition, prayer, and contemplation. Read and repeat each passage over and over as you seek to enter into the inner core of its truth. When sentiments arise in your heart, express them to Jesus in prayer (the third step). At times, you might experience God's presence in a way that brings you to speechless adoration. When contemplation resonates within you, your awareness will be enhanced. For now, after you have expressed your sentiments to Jesus, spend some time in silent adoration. Follow this format for each passage (text taken from Jn 9:1–38):

♦ They said to him then, "How were your eyes opened?" He answered, "That man they call Jesus made mud and smeared it on my eyes, telling me to go to Siloam and wash. When I did go and wash, I was able to see."

♦ "Since it was your eyes he opened, what do you have to say about him?" "He is a prophet," he replied.

♦ He came back at them: "Well, this is news! You do not know where he comes from, yet he opened my eyes. We know that God does not hear sinners, but that if someone is devout and obeys his will, he listens to him. It is unheard of that anyone ever gave sight to a person blind from birth. If this man were not from God, he could never have done such a thing."

♦ When Jesus heard of his expulsion, he sought him out and asked him, "Do you believe in the Son of Man?" He answered, "Who is he, sir, that I may believe in him?" "You have seen him," Jesus replied. "He is speaking to you now," "I do believe, Lord," he said, and bowed down to worship him.

▲ Reflection

The cure of the blind man's sight is a powerful testimony to Jesus' divine power and compassion. It is also a moving account of the man's developing discipleship, from a willingness to obey Jesus' command to wash himself in the pool of Siloam, to acknowledging in public that Jesus was the one who healed him, to witnessing to the Pharisees that Jesus was a prophet, to being expelled from the Synagogue for acknowledging Jesus as the Messiah, to bowing down in adoration of Jesus. Before our very eyes, this "sinner" and public outcast has become an ardent disciple and one of the beloved chosen.

Exercise Twelve
NEW LIFE IN HIS NAME

▲ Scripture

Jesus performed many other signs as well—signs not recorded here—in the presence of his disciples. But these have been recorded to help you believe that Jesus is the Messiah, the Son of God, so that through this faith you may have life in his name.

—John 20:30–31

▲ Summary

At the end of his gospel John offers this passage as a summary of Jesus' life and teachings. He explains that Jesus' miracles of healing and power were signs that Jesus came from God and was God. The resurrection is his greatest sign. Many were brought to heartfelt devotion of Jesus as their Savior and Lord either from personal experience or from eyewitness accounts of his miracles. There were those who refused to accept him as the Messiah and Son of God. Submission to Jesus would have meant their renunciation of the status quo. They shunned what they did not understand. Faith is the foundation, and commitment is the cornerstone, of our spiritual lives. The process of faith building involves dying to the old way of life and having "new life in his name."

▲ Session

(20–30 minute duration)

In this session you are going to assess to what degree Jesus has become your Messiah and Lord. To do this well you will need honesty, humility, and courage. You can ask some of the New Testament saints to intercede with the Holy Spirit on your behalf to increase your faith and help you to surrender to Jesus.

Along with Jesus, invite Jesus' mother, Joseph, Mary Magdalene, the man who received sight, Peter, and Thomas into your living room. Each of them saw Jesus and witnessed his signs. Each of them became his disciple. Ask them to share with you how they came to *see and accept* Jesus as their Savior and Lord. Ask also how, as their understanding deepened, the Lord's humanity became an *ineffable sign* of his divinity. Listen to each of them share their faith-story, beginning with the man healed of his blindness.

Now the spotlight is on you. In their presence, address your own relationship with Jesus. Talk about the milestones on this life-changing journey, as well as the pitfalls and obstacles that still remain in your path. Listen as each one of them shares with you a word of wisdom and encouragement, beginning with the man healed of his blindness, and ending with Jesus. As you engage Jesus, ask him earnestly to give you the grace to acknowledge him as your Savior and Lord in your every thought, word, and deed, and ask that your discipleship may always be joyous, honest, and courageous.

▲ Reflection

God's generosity toward us is incomprehensible. We are totally undeserving of God's love and salvation. More importantly, we can never acquire salvation on our own merits. God's salvation is offered freely to all of us. The wonder is that anyone who accepts Jesus as Savior and Lord experiences new life in him. God's loving touch changes lives dramatically. The Holy Spirit instills inexplicable joy and peace as we are guided and inspired. We are disciples and saints like the ones you invited into your living room. This destiny of living in God's embrace is yours!

How gentle and loving

your reminder to me,

in my heart where you secretly dwell

with your delightful breath

in glory and good will,

how soothingly do you woo me! [2]

Exercise Thirteen
FAITH KNOWS BEYOND UNDERSTANDING

▲ Scripture

Therefore the Lord himself will give you this sign: the virgin shall be with child, and bear a son, and shall name him Immanuel.

—Isaiah 7:14

When his mother Mary was engaged to Joseph, but before they lived together, she was found with child through the power of the Holy Spirit. Joseph her husband, an upright man unwilling to expose her to the law, decided to divorce her quietly. Such was his intention when suddenly the angel of the Lord appeared in a dream and said to him: "Joseph, son of David, have no fear about taking Mary as your wife. It is by the Holy Spirit that she has conceived this child. She is to have a son and you are to name him Jesus because he will save his people from their sins."

—Matthew 1:18b–21

▲ Summary

God's ways are not our ways. To our thinking a child can never be born to a virgin; nor should someone with such a questionable conception come from God. God's decisions call for our acquiescence, not because they conform to human thinking, but because God's intent is always true and reliable, even when it is beyond our understanding. Mary accepted the angel's word that her son would be conceived through the power of the Holy Spirit. Joseph took Mary to be his wife because he trusted the word given to him by God's messenger.

▲ Session

(20–30 minute duration)
You need a change of heart if the ways and will of God are to make sense to you. Only God can give you this wisdom

that is foolishness to the world. As you enter into your space with God, implore the Holy Spirit to make you transparent of heart so that you can believe the mystery of the Incarnation in full measure, the way Mary and Joseph did.

What better place to have your visit with God than at the manger? As you approach this humble cradle, ask the Holy Spirit to help you enter more deeply into the divine mystery incarnated in the baby Jesus.

Imagine yourself to be an active observer and participant as Mary and Joseph, along with the shepherds and the magi, recount their experiences of the birth of Jesus. Ask them questions and make comments as well, as you seek to fathom the depths of their faith-experiences. Spend as much time as you need in dialogue with each of them, knowing you can always return to continue the visit.

Finally, Mary gives you her child. Receive the child in your arms. In silence gaze lovingly and reverently at this tender, vulnerable baby who is your God and Savior. Try to express your sentiments of gratitude, joy, and wonder in words and then simply spend time in silent adoration.

▲ Reflection

There was no more intimate way of loving us than for God to become one of us. Such an act of selfless intimacy was offered to us in spite of the fact that we have reneged on our promises and been unfaithful to God. In taking upon himself the burden of our sins and atoning for them, Jesus made us worthy to claim him as our own brother. Such divine intimacy is a mystery that can only be understood in our hearts when the Holy Spirit reveals to us the wonder and holiness of God's designs.

Exercise Fourteen
FOR THOSE WHO ARE CALLED

▲ Scripture

Many Samaritans from that town believed in him on the strength of the woman's word of testimony. . . . The result was that . . . they begged him to stay with them awhile. So he stayed there two days, and through his own spoken word many more came to faith. As they told the woman: "No longer does our faith depend on your story. We have heard for ourselves, and we know that this really is the Savior of the world."

—John 4:39–42

▲ *Summary*

Assyria invaded Israel, the northern kingdom, and settled it with its own people (see 2 Kgs 17:24–41). The mixed race that developed became known as the Samaritans. "Purebred" Jews despised these "half-breeds," and the Samaritans in turn hated the Jews. Jesus held no such prejudices. He came to bring salvation to all, Jews and non-Jews alike. The Samaritan woman and her fellow villagers overcame their prejudices toward Jesus, a Jew. They accepted him as the Savior of the world because of the message of love and salvation he conveyed to them. No miracles were needed to convince them of his Godliness.

▲ *Session*

(20–30 minute duration)

Ask Jesus to give you the simple and childlike faith of the many Samaritans who believed in him on the strength of the woman's testimony. Then consider the conversion encounter between Jesus and the Samaritan woman:

◆ Jesus breaks an age-old tradition by asking for water from a Samaritan who is also a woman, thereby jolting her out of the fossilized parameters that society and tradition places upon them.

- Jesus leads her further into a faith-surrender. "If only you recognized God's gift, and who it is that is asking you for a drink, you would have asked him instead, and he would have given you living water" (Jn 4:10). At first she is the logical and practical one. Jesus does not have a bucket, so how can he provide her with water? But then, she wants to drink of this water and never be thirsty again.

- Jesus asks her to fetch her husband. She could lie to this stranger, but she chooses to be honest and says she has no husband. Jesus answers her, "You are right in saying that you have no husband! The fact is, you have had five, and the man you are living with now is not your husband. What you said is true" (Jn 4:17–18).

- The woman answers, "Sir, I can see you are a prophet. I know there is a Messiah coming. When he comes, he will tell us everything." Jesus replied, "I who speak to you am he" (Jn 4:25–26).

- The woman went off into the town and said to the people "Come and see someone who told me everything I ever did! Could this not be the Messiah?" (Jn 4:29). Jesus' words are a source of repentance, not condemnation.

End your prayer by conversing with Jesus about the sentiments aroused in you by this moving story of salvation. Ask him for insights into prejudices and resentments you may harbor. Seek the wisdom of his words for yourself as a source of repentance and freedom from condemnation.

▲ *Reflection*

This moving story shatters several prejudices. Who could have imagined the Samaritan woman would be open to conversion? Who could have thought those rigid prejudices between Jews and Samaritans would be broken down? Who could have thought that salvation would come to the Samaritans, who were religious outcasts? With God everything is possible and God can never be boxed in. Hope springs eternal because God is Emmanuel. God's dream of restoration and renewal is for all.

Exercise Fifteen
JESUS, THE BREAD OF LIFE

▲ *Scripture*

"I am the bread of life. Your ancestors ate manna in the desert, but they died. This is the bread that comes down from heaven for a man to eat and never die. I myself am the living bread come down from heaven. If anyone eats this bread he shall live forever; the bread I will give is my flesh, for the life of the world."

—John 6:48–51

▲ *Summary*

Jesus' words convey God's mystery that taxes our human understanding. Jesus demands our surrender in faith and total trust. To those who surrender themselves, Jesus' words and actions make joyous and transforming sense. Jesus becomes the bread of life to them and they experience everlasting life here on earth. As for those who reject Jesus' words, their relationship to God remains egocentric and unproductive.

▲ *Session*

(20–30 minute duration)

In John 6, Jesus reveals his deepest desire for what he wants us to be: the beloved companion who eats bread with him. Yet, indeed, he himself is our bread. Ask him to give you a deep sense of joyous wonder and humble reverence as you ponder with him the mystery of the Eucharist. You can use the *lectio divina* method of prayer.

♦ "I myself am the bread of life. No one who comes to me shall ever be hungry, no one who believes in me shall ever thirst. But as I told you—though you have seen me, you still do not believe" (Jn 6:35–36).

- "Indeed, this is the will of my Father, that everyone who looks upon the Son and believes in him shall have eternal life. Him I will raise up on the last day" (Jn 6:40).

- "I am the bread of life. Your ancestors ate manna in the desert, but they died. This is the bread that comes down from heaven for a man to eat and never die" (Jn 48–50).

- "I myself am the living bread come down from heaven. If anyone eats this bread he shall live forever; the bread I will give is my flesh, for the life of the world" (Jn 6:51).

- "Let me solemnly assure you, if you do not eat the flesh of the Son of Man and drink his blood, you have no life in you. He who feeds on my flesh and drinks my blood has life eternal and I will raise him up on the last day" (Jn 6:53–54).

- From this time on, many of his disciples broke away and would not remain in his company any longer. Jesus then said to the Twelve, "Do you want to leave me too?" Simon Peter answered him, "Lord, to whom shall we go? You have the words of eternal life. We have come to believe; we are convinced that you are God's holy one." (Jn 6:66–69).

Finally, share with Jesus the sentiments and movements the Holy Spirit has evoked in your heart as you pondered Jesus being your living bread and eternal sustenance.

▲ *Reflection*

The Eucharist is sacrifice and sustenance. Jesus is the innocent lamb whose blood has been shed in perfect atonement of our sins. He is also the Passover Lamb that is eaten in remembrance of God's salvation in him. Jesus has become our *viaticum*, our life-giving food along the journey to eternal life. We have eternal life and will be raised up on the last day because we have taken him as our Bread of Life.

Exercise Sixteen
JESUS, THE LAMB OF GOD

▲ Scripture

Like a lamb led to the slaughter or a sheep before the shearers, he was silent and opened not his mouth.
—Isaiah 53:7

"Worthy are you [the lamb] to receive the scroll and break open its seals, for you were slain. With your blood you purchased for God, men of every race and tongue, of every people and nation. You made of them a kingdom, and priests to serve our God, and they shall reign on the earth."
—Revelation 5:9–10

The next day, when John caught sight of Jesus coming toward him, he exclaimed: "Look! There is the Lamb of God who takes away the sin of the world!"
—John 1:29

▲ Summary

John the Baptizer identifies Jesus as the Lamb of God who takes away the sins of the world. For the Israelites to be spared from the plague of death at the time of the Exodus a lamb with no defects had to be killed and its blood placed on the doorframes of each home. In killing this chosen lamb, the Israelites shed innocent blood. The lamb was a sacrifice, a substitute for the person who would have died in the plague. From then on, the Hebrew people understood that for them to be spared from death, an innocent life had to be sacrificed in their place. The lamb's blood foreshadowed the blood of Christ, the Lamb of God, who gave his life for the sins of all people.

▲ Session

(20–30 minute duration)
In our Scripture passages, Jesus tells us clearly who he is: the Lamb of God who takes away the sins of the world. Ask the Holy Spirit to give you a deeper sense of your sins and

humbly ask forgiveness as you prepare for your visit with Jesus.

Ponder very deliberately the following reflections and talk to Jesus about the various conclusions you have drawn from them:

♦ You can only address Jesus as the Lamb of God if, in the depths of your heart, you are convinced that you are a sinner. *Do you truly believe you are a sinner and will henceforth refrain from making excuses and offering alibis?*

♦ You can only address Jesus as the Lamb of God if you truly believe that you cannot save yourself and need Jesus as your Savior. *Do you believe you have given up the illusion that you can save yourself?*

♦ You can only address Jesus as the Lamb of God if you believe that the depths of God's mystery are revealed in the acknowledgment of your sins. *When you sin, do you flee from God, or run into his embrace?*

♦ You can only address Jesus as the Lamb of God if you are willing to embrace his worldview as envisioned in the Beatitudes: dependence on God in everything, commitment to a life of simplicity and humility, God-centeredness and mercy, and embracing persecution for Jesus' sake. *Are you willing to live your life in this way?*

▲ Reflection

Fittingly, the Church offers us a wonderful preparation for receiving the Body and Blood of Jesus at Eucharist. Twice we implore the Lamb of God who takes away the sins of the world to have mercy on us. Then we ask the same Lamb of God to grant us peace. Peace is the fruit of God's mercy and forgiveness. Peace comes to all who have repented and allowed God to "raise [us] on high" (Jas 4:10).

Exercise Seventeen
JESUS, GOD'S SON AND CHOSEN ONE

▲ Scripture

. . . He took Peter, John and James, and went up onto a mountain to pray. While he was praying, his face changed in appearance and his clothes became dazzlingly white. Suddenly two men were talking with him—Moses and Elijah. They appeared in glory and spoke of his passage, which he was about to fulfill in Jerusalem. . . . While Peter was speaking, a cloud came and overshadowed them, and the disciples grew fearful as the others entered it. Then from the cloud came a voice which said, "This is my Son, my Chosen One. Listen to him."

—Luke 9:28–31; 34–35

▲ Summary

Moses and Elijah were chosen by God. They were divinely designated to articulate for God the purpose and intent of the divine dream. As witnesses of God's power and holiness, they were transformed. They were human beings who served God well and acted as forerunners of the Messiah who would come from God and make manifest "God among us." In the transfiguration, Jesus offers us another clear sign that indeed he is God's Son, the Chosen One. He brings to fulfillment the work of salvation God began through the prophets of old.

▲ Session

(20–30 minute duration)
As you prepare to enter into your holy space with God, where transformation occurs, ask the Holy Spirit to touch your heart and move your spirit, so that God's designs for you might truly become manifest.

Imagine you are at the scene of the Transfiguration along with Peter, James, and John. As you trudge up the mountain with this select group, enjoy this intimate moment with

Jesus. You have heard of his miracles and teaching from eyewitness accounts; they indicate to you that Jesus is from God. On the mountaintop you become an eyewitness to Jesus' transfiguration. He is changed before your very eyes. His face becomes as dazzling as the sun, his clothes as radiant as light. Suddenly Moses and Elijah appear. Watch with Peter, James, and John as Moses and Elijah converse with Jesus.

Peter is overwhelmed with wonder and talks about erecting three booths, one for Jesus, one for Moses, and one for Elijah. He doesn't seem to know what he is talking about. Suddenly a bright cloud overshadows all of you, and out of the cloud you hear the Father's voice, "This is my beloved Son on whom my favor rests. Listen to him." Upon hearing this voice you are overwhelmed with fear and you lay down with your face to the ground. Then Jesus lays his hand on you and tells you to get up and not be afraid.

Stay in the divine presence of Jesus and dedicate your love and service to Him who is your Savior and your God.

▲ Reflection

Jesus always seems to take us boldly and gently, step by step, into the process of transformation. The purpose of transformation is always that we are moved toward focusing our every thought, word, and deed on Christ. By pondering his teaching and miracles, we learn that he is much more than what meets the eye. He is indeed the Christ, the Messiah, God's Son, and the Chosen One.

Through his humanity Jesus became God among us. Many came to recognize, albeit slowly, that his divinity was genuine, as evidenced in the transfiguration and resurrection. In like fashion, Jesus reveals himself to each of us in his acknowledgment of who we truly are, loving and accepting us where we are. Gradually his saving presence transforms us into new creations, God's own daughters and sons. The calling is to be holy, blameless, and full of love. Surely we are called to be Christ to one another, to carry on his presence among us.

Exercise Eighteen
SPIRITUALITY OF THE GOOD SAMARITAN

▲ Scripture

"Which of these three, in your opinion, was neighbor to the man who fell in with the robbers?" The answer came, "The one who treated him with compassion." Jesus said to him, "Then go and do the same."
—Luke 10:36–37

▲ Summary

In offering the parable of the Good Samaritan, Jesus dispels the narrow notion that salvation is offered only to a select few. In fact, salvation is a universal gift and humans of every race, color, and language are sons and daughters of God. Further, we need to shed our prejudices and realize that virtuous deeds and holy endeavors can and do come from the most unexpected quarters, as in the case of the Samaritan man.

▲ Session

(20–30 minute duration)
Take a few moments to prepare yourself for your visit with Jesus by asking the Holy Spirit to anoint your mind and heart so that you are truly open to God's ways and designs.

Imagine you are the Jewish traveler journeying from Jerusalem to Jericho. You fall prey to robbers who strip you, beat you, and then take off, leaving you to die alone on the roadside. You are stricken with anguish and pain and quite desperate about your survival. A spark of hope ignites within you as you see a priest coming your way. You are confident he will help you, as he is a man of God. Your hope crumbles into despair as he takes notice of your plight yet continues on. While you are in the throes of death, a Levite comes along. Once again your spirit awakens, but your expectation is tempered with doubt. You are devastated when the Levite sees you and decides not to help. By now you are convinced that death will be your next visitor.

Just then you notice that a Samaritan man is coming your way. For centuries the Samaritans have been the enemy of your people and you can sense all your distaste toward him surfacing within you. You are also fearful, as you are so vulnerable. Still, a flicker of hope arises in you. Will it too be extinguished? Do you dare imagine that this "enemy" will help you in your need?

On seeing you, the Samaritan is moved to compassion. He approaches you, dresses your wounds, pouring in oil and wine to soothe and comfort you in your distress. He then lifts you onto his own animal and brings you to an inn, where he cares for you. The next day he pays the innkeeper to look after you till he returns. What is the conversation you have with the Samaritan when he returns and pays the innkeeper for any further expense?

Spend time with Jesus as you examine your own attitudes toward people. And talk to Jesus about whether or not you have allowed him to be the Good Samaritan to you.

▲ Reflection

The parable of the Good Samaritan is told to a people who long believed that salvation was the product of a strict adherence to rules and regulations, the result of one's hard work and merit. Repentance and salvation from God had no place in such a scheme. The Samaritan, whose beliefs stood in direct contrast, could only be viewed with prejudice. Yet by Jesus' standards, the Samaritan was God's messenger indeed. In bringing the gift of restored life to the unfortunate traveler, he was himself saved. Go, and do the same!

Exercise Nineteen
WHO DO YOU SAY THAT I AM?

▲ *Scripture*

... [Jesus] asked his disciples this question: "Who do people say that the Son of Man is?" They replied, "Some say John the Baptizer, others Elijah, still others Jeremiah or one of the prophets." "And you," he said to them, "who do you say that I am?" "You are the Messiah," Simon Peter answered, "the Son of the living God!"

—Matthew 16:13–16

▲ *Summary*

Jesus is slowly becoming more than a curiosity and sideshow attraction. Although a strange phenomenon, he is beginning to be taken seriously. He is likened to John the Baptizer, Elijah, and Jeremiah or one of the prophets. His spiritual status is rising, and he is seen as a prophet who speaks on God's behalf, as did the others before him. In this passage Jesus challenges the faith of his disciples in him. He wants them to go farther than his human nature. Peter's response indicates that Jesus' divinity is slowly beginning to be recognized and accepted, although, as subsequent events will make clear, the disciples have a long way to go.

▲ *Session*

(20–30 minute duration)
In this session you will prepare yourself to address honestly the question Jesus is posing: "Who do you say that I am?" Ask St. Peter to intercede for you as you search the depths of your relationship with Jesus for your answer.

Visit with a group of individuals from the New Testament who encountered this same question in their discipleship, and discuss with them their various responses.

♦ There is Peter, who acknowledged Jesus as his Savior and Lord and later denied him. However, his discipleship matured because Jesus never gave up on him. He rose to great heights, and was asked by Jesus to lead his Church and give his life for the New Way.

♦ Thomas is present, ardent and stubborn in his discipleship. His vision of the Messiah clashed with the unfolding events of Jesus' life, leading to his passion and death. Thomas was so disillusioned that he did not dare believe that the resurrection was possible. To Thomas's mind, the resurrection was not even an option. Let him tell you about his encounter with the risen Jesus.

♦ Nicodemus acknowledged that Jesus was a teacher come from God, for no man could perform signs and wonders such as Jesus performed unless God was with him (Jn 3:1–21). Jesus invited Nicodemus to go beyond this and recognize that Jesus is more than a prophet. Indeed, he is the Son of God and whoever believes in him will not die but will have eternal life. Nicodemus later accompanied Joseph of Arimathea and anointed Jesus' dead body for burial (Jn 19:39). Listen to him tell his story of discipleship as it moves from secret acceptance of Jesus to open acknowledgment.

♦ Judas, who was in charge of the money, is here. He was invited to close intimacy with Jesus; he chose instead to live the lie. In the end he could not believe that Jesus could forgive him for his betrayal so he ended his life in shame and despair.

♦ Finally, visit with Jesus and talk to him about what you have learned from his other disciples. Share with him what you have learned about your own discipleship.

▲ *Reflection*

James tells us, "faith without works is as dead as a body without breath" (Jas 2:26). We know we have truly accepted Jesus as our Savior and Lord when our lives and actions build up the body of Christ. True profession of faith in Jesus leads to a public acknowledgment of him as well as a strong commitment to stewardship of God's people.

Exercise Twenty
JESUS, THE SOURCE OF SALVATION

▲ Scripture

While they were still speaking about all this, he him-self stood in their midst [and said to them, "Peace to you."] In their panic and fright they thought they were seeing a ghost. He said to them, "Why are you disturbed? Why do such ideas cross your mind? Look at my hands and my feet; it is really I. Touch me, and see that a ghost does not have flesh and bones as I do." As he said this he showed them his hands and feet. They were still incredulous for sheer joy and wonder, so he said to them, "Have you any-thing here to eat?" They gave him a piece of cooked fish, which he took and ate in their presence. Then he said to them, "Recall those words I spoke to you when I was still with you: everything written about me in the law of Moses and the prophets and psalms had to be fulfilled." Then he opened their minds to the understanding of the Scriptures.

—Luke 24:36–45

▲ Summary

The risen Lord's presence is so overwhelming to the disci-ples that "they were still incredulous for sheer joy and won-der." No other words could better capture their hang-time experience, suspended between heaven and earth. Jesus is their bridge, incarnating heaven on earth. Stepping out onto that bridge, they experience a piece of heaven while they still inhabit the dwelling place of mortals. From then on they understand that the heavenly blessings are within reach of all God's children.

▲ Session

(20–30 minute duration)
You are about to have a face-to-face visit with your risen Lord and Savior. Imagine you are in an antechamber and

ask the Holy Spirit to give you the proper dispositions for this forthcoming apparition of the risen Lord to you.

You are with the eleven disciples as Jesus appears to you. Jesus appears to all of you and greets you with his peace. Your first reaction to his presence is one of panic and fright. Your eyes of faith have not yet been opened; you think you are seeing a ghost. Jesus then invites you to look at his hands and feet. Now as a group you have a wonderfully strange response, you are incredulous for sheer joy and wonder. You know you are in the saving presence of the risen Jesus. He then eats a piece of cooked fish and sums up the whole purpose of his life: "Recall those words I spoke to you when I was still with you: everything written about me in the law of Moses and the prophets and psalms had to be fulfilled." Finally, he opens your minds to the understanding of the Scriptures.

Jesus then takes you aside and the two of you spend time with each other. Express your adoration and gratitude and ask for the grace of generosity and joy as you strive to walk in the footsteps of your Master.

▲ *Reflection*

The resurrection made right all that was still incomplete in the faith and dependence of the disciples on their Master and Lord. After the resurrection, Peter and the other disciples went forth in joy and confidence, spreading the Good News that Jesus was the Savior of Jew and Gentile alike. The Resurrection of Jesus is God's clearest sign of total victory over sin and Satan. Faith in the risen Jesus makes us heirs of the kingdom of God and the object of God's dream of restoration and renewal.

CHAPTER GLEANINGS

▲ It seems rather astonishing, given the unfaithful history of God's people, that our Lord continually hopes and dreams that we will come to live in Christ's image. Yet such is the power of God's salvation through Jesus. This is the transformation that takes place in any individual who, like the blind man, accepts Jesus as Savior and Lord, and humbles his or her entire being in submission to Him as the Son of the living God.

▲ God's generosity toward us is incomprehensible. We are totally undeserving of God's love and salvation. More importantly, we can never acquire salvation on our own merits. God's salvation is offered freely to all of us. The wonder is that anyone who accepts Jesus as Savior and Lord experiences new life in him. God's loving touch changes lives dramatically.

▲ God's decisions call for our acquiescence, not because they conform to human thinking but because God's intent is always true and reliable, even when it is beyond our understanding.

▲ To those who have surrendered themselves, Jesus' words and actions make joyous and transforming sense. Jesus becomes the bread of life to them and they experience everlasting life here on earth. Those who have rejected Jesus' words, however, remain egocentric and unproductive, even in their relationship to God.

▲ After the resurrection, Peter and the other disciples went forth in joy and confidence, spreading the Good News that Jesus is the Savior of Jew and Gentile alike. The Resurrection of Jesus is God's clearest sign of total victory over sin and Satan. Faith in the risen Jesus makes us heirs of the kingdom of God and the object of God's dream of restoration and renewal.

CHAPTER THREE

God's Dream—
Brought to Completion in the Holy Spirit

In the fourteenth chapter of his Gospel, John portrays Jesus offering his last discourse to his disciples. As on other occasions, Jesus is surrounded by his intimate circle of friends and followers. This time, however, there is a sense of urgency. Soon Jesus will be going to his crucifixion and death. Before his departure he shares some of his deepest yearnings and promises for his flock saying,

> "I will ask the Father and he will give you another Paraclete—to be with you always: the Spirit of truth, whom the world cannot accept, since it neither sees him nor recognizes him; but you can recognize him because he remains with you and will be within you. I will not leave you orphaned; I will come back to you" (Jn 14:16–18).

PROMISE OF THE HOLY SPIRIT

In offering us the gift of his Spirit, Jesus makes a sublime promise. He mentions several descriptive details about the Spirit in order to give us a deeper appreciation of this gift. The Spirit will be *another* Advocate, implying that Jesus is the first Advocate. The Spirit will continue the same kind of advocacy that Jesus began. In the Greek understanding, an advocate is a person who stands with his hand on your shoulder, signifying that he is there to protect and defend you. In legal parlance, he is your defender rather than the prosecutor. The Holy Spirit will continue this awesome task of defending us before the throne of God, making the case that the divine plan to make us sons and daughters of the living God is proper and fitting and that, by God's grace and mercy, we are made worthy because of who God is.

THE INDWELLING SPIRIT

Jesus describes the Holy Spirit as *dwelling among us*. This is another instance where the term *Emmanuel* is applied to God. It was first used by Isaiah when he predicted the birth of the Messiah: ". . . The virgin shall be with child, and bear a son, and shall name him Immanuel" (Is 7:14). Matthew turns to the same quotation when describing the birth of Jesus, except that he represents the meaning of Emmanuel as "God is with us" (Mt 1:23). There is no more expressive name than Emmanuel to bring out the significance of the incarnation, God's intimate design of making union with the divinity irresistible for us. The humanity of Jesus becomes *the way* for us to probe the depths of God's mystery. This same name *Emmanuel* is now applied to the Holy Spirit.

Jesus goes further in describing the function and purpose of the Holy Spirit in our lives. The Divine Spirit dwells not only among us as Emmanuel, but also *within us.* The Spirit will become the keeper of the disciple's soul, that most intimate place in our beings where we savor our most precious treasures and memories. It is in our hearts that we hold sacred our family members and friends. Of all these treasures and gifts, the Holy Spirit will be the most significant and precious. Like Jesus, the Holy Spirit will be an intimate part of our lives, becoming the guest of our souls, dwelling in our innermost beings. Jesus tells us that the world (people who do not share the spirit of Jesus) will not be able to recognize the presence of the Holy Spirit in their lives because they are paying heed to other spirits.

TUTORED BY THE HOLY SPIRIT

Delving further into John 14, we observe that Jesus instructs his disciples that "the Paraclete, the Holy Spirit whom the Father will send in my name, will instruct you in everything, and remind you of all that I told you" (Jn 14:26). Jesus allays any doubts we might have about the eventual outcome of his mission. His mission of bringing salvation to the world through his death and resurrection, making us sons and daughters of the living God, and establishing God's reign in our midst, *will be brought to completion.* And this will happen through the power and workings of the Holy Spirit who will occupy a central place in our lives. Through the Holy Spirit, the presence and essence of Jesus is formed and strengthened in us. The reign of God bears fruit and is made perfect through the inspiration and leadership of the Holy Spirit. The Church then is the era of the Holy Spirit.

INFUSED BY THE SPIRIT

The Book of Acts is a powerful testimony to the dynamism of the Holy Spirit in the lives of Jesus' followers. We are told in the second chapter that the day of Pentecost found the disciples gathered in one place.

> Suddenly from up in the sky there came a noise like a strong, driving wind which was heard all through the house where they were seated. Tongues as of fire appeared, which parted and came to rest on each of them. All were filled with the Holy Spirit. They began to express themselves in foreign tongues and make bold proclamation as the Spirit prompted them (Acts 2:2–4).

From that point on the saving power of God is made manifest through the workings of the Holy Spirit in the lives of the disciples, as they form a community in Jesus' name. They make confident proclamations as prompted by the Spirit. They express themselves boldly in foreign tongues that they themselves do not understand. With great freedom and enthusiasm Peter openly witnesses to the life and resurrection of Jesus, proclaiming,

> ". . . God has made both Lord and Messiah this Jesus whom you crucified. . . . You must reform and be baptized, each one of you, in the name of Jesus Christ, that your sins may be forgiven; then you will receive the gift of the Holy Spirit. It was to you and your children that the promise was made, and to all those still far off whom the Lord our God calls" (Acts 2:36, 38–39).

TRANSFORMED BY THE POWER OF THE HOLY SPIRIT

A great transformation has taken place in the disciples. Before Jesus' passion and death they were fearful, confused, and uncomprehending of much of what Jesus imparted to them. After his death, their sorrow and devastation was overwhelming. Their state of mind was summed up in several of their reactions. John tells us that the disciples had locked the doors of the place where they were for fear of the Jews (20:19). The disciples on their way to Emmaus had been "hoping that he was the one who would set Israel free" (Lk 24:21). Yet even though they knew that some among them had received a vision of angels telling them that Jesus had risen from the dead, they could not believe without seeing. Their hope was dying in their despair. When Thomas was told by the others that they had seen the Lord, his answer was, "I will never believe it without probing the nail-prints in his hands, without putting my finger in the nail marks and my hand into his side" (Jn 20:25). Jesus obliged him with a special apparition and satisfied all his demands. He also rebuked him gently by telling him not to persist in his unbelief, but believe. These same disciples were emboldened by the Holy Spirit. They were transformed beyond recognition, as members of the Sanhedrin soon found out.

STEPPING INTO JESUS' FOOTSTEPS

The transformation of the community, and especially of Peter and Paul, is described in detail in Acts.

After the cure of the cripple in Chapter Three, Peter is a fearless witness before the Sanhedrin. Gone are his timidity and vacillation. When he is questioned about the cure of the cripple, his lack of education and social standing do not deter him from answering boldly, ". . . It was done in the name of Jesus Christ the Nazorean whom you crucified and whom God raised from the dead. . . . There is no salvation in anyone else" . . . (Acts 4:10a, 12a).

The power of the Holy Spirit to transform hearts is evident when we remember that just a short time before, this same Peter was afraid to admit even knowing who Jesus was to a servant girl in the outer courtyard. Now, standing before the Sanhedrin, Peter is unflinching. When they warn him to stop speaking and teaching about Jesus, he is beyond intimidation and falsehood and answers, "Judge for yourselves whether it is right in God's sight for us to obey you rather than God. Surely we cannot help speaking of what we have heard and seen" (Acts 4:19–20).

Later in Acts we observe that the power of the Holy Spirit continues to be at work through Peter.

The people carried the sick into the streets and laid them on cots and mattresses so that when Peter passed by at least his shadow might fall on one or another of them. Crowds from the towns around Jerusalem would gather, too, bringing their sick and those who were troubled by unclean spirits, all of whom were cured (Acts 5:15–16).

The Christian community prayed that God would "[stretch forth his] hand in cures and signs and wonders to be worked in the name of Jesus" as a way of assuring the truth of the message they continued to proclaim (Acts 4:30).

Peter also continues to be questioned and threatened by the Sanhedrin. In response to the authority's restrictions and threats, the apostles proclaimed:

"Better for us to obey God than men! . . . He whom God has exalted at his right hand as ruler and savior is to bring repentance to Israel and forgiveness of sins. We testify to this. So too does the Holy Spirit, whom God has given to those that obey him" (Acts 5:29, 31–32).

When many members of the Sanhedrin were ready to put the apostles to death, the voice of reason prevailed in the person of Gamaliel. His words zoomed in on the manifest power of the Holy Spirit and the utter futility of working against God. He said, "My advice is that you have nothing to do with these men. Let them alone. If their purpose or activity is human in its origins, it will destroy itself. If, on the other hand, it comes from God, you will not be able to destroy them without fighting God himself" (Acts 5:38–39). The apostles were flogged, ordered not to speak again about the name of Jesus, and dismissed—yet the remainder of the Book of Acts attests to their continued efforts to share the story of the resurrection.

PERSECUTOR MADE APOSTLE

In Acts Chapter Seven, Saul witnessed and participated in the stoning death of Stephen. In Chapter Nine Saul is described as an ardent and violent zealot, spouting murderous threats against the Lord's disciples, asking for letters from the high priests to the synagogues in Damascus so that he could arrest and bring to Jerusalem any members of the Christian community he could find. The story of his conversion is among the most dramatic in the history of the church.

> As he traveled along and was approaching Damascus, a light from the sky suddenly flashed about him. He fell to the ground and at the same time heard a voice say, "Saul, Saul, why do you persecute me?" "Who are you, sir?" he asked. The voice answered, "I am Jesus, the one you are persecuting. Get up and go into the city, where you will be told what to do." The men who were traveling with him stood there speechless. They had heard the voice but could see no one. Saul got up from the ground unable to see, even though his eyes were open. They had to take him by the hand and lead him into Damascus. For three days he continued blind, during which time he neither ate nor drank (Acts 9:3–9).

Jesus asked Ananias, a disciple, to minister to Saul. Understandably, Ananias protested that Saul was a dangerous man who had wreaked havoc on the followers of the New Way. Jesus persuaded Ananias to do his bidding, as he had chosen Saul to be his instrument of salvation, to bring Jesus' message to the Gentiles and the people of Israel. When Ananias came to baptize Saul, "Immediately something like scales fell from his eyes and he regained his sight. He got up and was baptized, and his strength returned to him after he had taken food" (Acts 9:18–19a).

PASSIONATE IN THE MASTER'S SERVICE

Filled with the power of the Holy Spirit, Paul dedicates his life to being an apostle of Jesus Christ, bringing the Good News of salvation to one and all. He undertakes three missionary journeys on which he preaches to Jews and Gentiles alike. He and his companions make converts and are persecuted for their commitment to Jesus.

Paul establishes communities of believers in places like Phillipi, Thessalonica, and Beroea. He is tireless in the service of his Master. Throughout his ministry, Paul has great success preaching the Gospel to the Gentile world. During his third missionary journey, the narrative in Acts reflects a certain restlessness and uneasiness on Paul's part. He has a growing conviction that the Spirit is calling him to Jerusalem in preparation for bringing the message of the New Way to Rome. He senses that imprisonment and suffering will be his lot in Jerusalem. After suffering persecution and imprisonment in Jerusalem, he wins his appeal to be tried in Rome, as he is a Roman citizen. The Book of Acts ends with an account of Paul under house arrest in Rome for two full years. During this time, "With full assurance, and without any hindrance whatever, he preached the reign of God and taught about the Lord Jesus Christ" (Acts 28:31).

TRANSFORMED BY THE SPIRIT

In his apostolic journeys and ministry to various Christian communities, Paul endures much opposition. During the course of his apostleship he is able to clarify his understanding of Jesus' teachings and the workings of the Holy Spirit. In his letter to the Galatians, Paul emphasizes two important dimensions of Jesus' mission: justification through faith and the proper use of freedom, or living under the guidance and mentoring of the Holy Spirit.

As an educated and well-informed Pharisee, Paul is steeped in the Law and believes that justification comes from the observance of the Law. As a Christian, Paul begins to build his understanding of the gift of salvation around the question of man's justification before God: ". . . a man is not justified by legal observance but by faith in Jesus Christ . . ." (Gal 2:16). He goes on to say that "the life I live now is not my own; Christ is living in me. I still live my human life, but it is a life of faith in the Son of God, who loved me and gave himself for me. I will not treat God's gracious gift as pointless" (Gal 2:20–21a).

Justification in Jesus Christ leads to true freedom. Paul draws a sharp contrast between the fruits of the flesh and the fruits of the Spirit:

It is obvious what proceeds from the flesh: lewd conduct, impurity, licentiousness, idolatry, sorcery, hostilities, bickering, jealousy, outbursts of rage, selfish rivalries, dissensions, factions, envy, drunkenness, orgies, and the like. I warn you as I have warned you before: those who do such things will not inherit the kingdom of God! (Gal 5:19–21).

In contrast, the fruits of the Spirit are love, joy, peace, patient endurance, kindness, generosity, faith, mildness, and chastity. Against such there is no law! Those who belong to Christ Jesus have crucified their flesh with its passions and desires. Since we live by the spirit, let us follow the spirit's lead. Let us never be boastful, or challenging, or jealous toward one another (Gal 5:22–26).

God's action is clear in the fruits of the Spirit: once again God brings order and harmony out of the chaos and turmoil of our hearts.

FALLING IN LOVE WITH THE HOLY SPIRIT

Throughout the history of Christian discipleship, holy men and women have excelled in the formation imparted to them through the Holy Spirit. The Holy Spirit became a real and loving presence in their lives, guiding them in their everyday decisions and activities and leading them into the heart of God's mystery. People like Saint Antony of the Desert, Saint Benedict, Saint Francis of Assisi, Saint Catherine of Siena, Saint Ignatius of Loyola, Saint Teresa of Avila, and Saint John of the Cross have given us marvelous insights as to how the Holy Spirit works in our lives. Here are some of their conclusions:

- ▲ The gift of discernment flows from the disciple's passionate commitment to live according to Jesus' teachings.

- ▲ Commitment is about serving God through service of God's people. True love expresses itself in deeds (see 1 Jn 3:18).

- When the opposing spirit is moving within us creating desolation, it is important to counter it with boldness. Any form of secrecy needs to be exposed. A good spiritual director or companion is always a great help.

- It is not enough to be generous in the spiritual life. One needs to develop wisdom that only the Holy Spirit can give. The disciple is constantly alert, even when all seems to be going well. Those who seek God's will in everyday life soon learn that they can never let their spiritual guard down. Vigilance, in both consolation and desolation, is the price of true discipleship (see 1 Pt 5:8–9).

- Discernment is a gift and a task. It is a gift that the Holy Spirit will grant us if we ask assiduously for it. It is a task because the Holy Spirit desires our cooperation in making every effort to do God's will in our lives.

- Constant companionship with the Holy Spirit, during formal prayer and during the day's events, will create a discerning lifestyle in the disciple.

Exercise Twenty-One
SHELTERED IN THE SPIRIT

▲ Scripture

Mary said to the angel, "How can this be since I do not know man?" The angel answered her: "The Holy Spirit will come upon you and the power of the Most High will overshadow you; hence, the holy offspring to be born will be called Son of God. . . . Mary said: "I am the servant of the Lord. Let it be done to me as you say."
—Luke 1:34–35, 38

▲ Summary

Perhaps the most enduring quality of deeply committed Christians is their total obedience to God's intentions, even when it threatens the very fabric of their existence. Trust is the bedrock of their relationship with God. Mary was God's handmaid, always at her Lord's beck and call. She was plunged into a pregnancy outside wedlock that could have resulted in death by stoning, as was customary under the Law. The angel told her she would be with child by the power of the Holy Spirit. God turned her world topsy-turvy, making possible the impossible.

▲ Session

(20–30 minute duration)

Ask the Holy Spirit to soften your heart into loving generously and to mold your will into submission so that God's intentions and yearnings for you become yours as well.

Mary walked in the footsteps laid out for her. Every divine wish became her command. Along with Elizabeth, try to assimilate Mary's experience of the angel's visitation and her ponderings about it in her Canticle:

♦ The angel Gabriel tells her that the Holy Spirit will come upon her and the power of the Most High will overshadow her. Hence the holy offspring to be born will be called the Son of God. *Explore with Mary how she experienced God's intervention in her life and what it was* like to carry the Son of God in her womb for nine months.

♦ "My being proclaims the greatness of the Lord; my spirit finds joy in God my savior, for he has looked upon his servant in her lowliness" (Lk 1:46b–48a). *How often have you said the same about your own life and circumstances? Spend some time proclaiming the Lord's greatness for the many gifts and blessings you have received. Try naming them individually.*

♦ "God who is mighty has done great things for me, holy is his name; his mercy is from age to age on those who fear him" (Lk 1:49–50). *Has God become first and foremost in all you think, say and do? Assess your relationship with your Savior. Assuming no mercy is possible without our honest acknowledgment of sin and willingness to forgive others, what is the correlation between your transparency and God's mercy toward you?*

♦ "He has deposed the mighty from their thrones and raised the lowly to high places. The hungry he has given every good thing, while the rich he has sent empty away" (Lk 1:52–53). *Do you understand this lowliness and hunger Mary is talking about? Have you been lowly and raised, hungry and given every good thing? Ask the Holy Spirit for Mary's radical dependence on God.*

Finally, come before the Holy Trinity and spend time in quiet adoration and praise of your Creator and Lord. Petition the Trinity for the grace of making them your *only* Absolute.

▲ Reflection

There seems to be no more appropriate way of crystallizing Mary's single-minded devotion to her God than by relishing the inspired encomium her cousin Elizabeth gave her at their meeting: ". . . Blest are you among women and blest is the fruit of your womb. . . . The moment your greeting sounded in my ears, the baby leapt in my womb for joy. Blest is she who trusted that the Lord's words to her would be fulfilled" (Lk 1:42, 44–45). Mary was overshadowed by the Most High and in return enwombed the Most High for the rest of her life.

Exercise Twenty-Two
THE SPIRIT DWELLS IN THE TEMPLE

▲ Scripture

"If you love me and obey the commands I give you, I will ask the Father and he will give you another Paraclete—to be with you always: the Spirit of truth, whom the world cannot accept, since it neither sees him nor recognizes him; but you can recognize him because he remains with you and will be within you."

—John 14:15–17

▲ Summary

Jesus promises us another Advocate, he being the first one by implication. This Advocate is the Spirit of Truth. *Advocate* is synonymous with someone who stands by our side speaking on our behalf and giving us comfort and reassurance. It is an enormous consolation to hear Jesus tell us that he will ask the Father to send us another Counselor who will bear the same marks of divine compassion and passionate longing to bring us home into the Heavenly Father's bosom. This Holy Spirit will remain with us, becoming another Emmanuel. This Paraclete will dwell within us, making us God's temples.

▲ Session

(20–30 minute duration)
In this session you are going to review the Holy Spirit's workings in your heart. Ask that your heart be filled with gratitude and joy at the way God has chosen to love and care for you. Imagine you are with Jesus in a place conducive to intimate conversation: it could be your living room, or a sacred place in nature, or in church.

Jesus is addressing you directly: *"If you love me and obey the commands I give you, I will ask the Father and he will give you another Paraclete —to be with you always: the Spirit of truth."* Jesus is asking you as he asked his disciples,

"Who am I for you?" What do you have to say? Which commands do you obey readily? With which commands do you have particular difficulty? To what extent has God's Spirit become the Spirit of Truth in you? What do you hear the Spirit of Truth saying to you? If the Spirit of Truth is not recognizable by the world, in what way are you not of the world?

Now spend time with the Holy Spirit as you search the depths of your relationship with the Third Person. Jesus says, *"You can recognize him because he remains with you and will be within you."* It is only family and close friends who remain with us, sharing the intimate gift of self. Are you as familiar and personal with the Holy Spirit as you are with your own flesh and blood?

And, not surprisingly, Jesus tells us that God's Spirit will be within us. Has the Holy Spirit become as familiar to you as your breath? Are you as intimate with the Holy Spirit as you are with your limbs, sense faculties, intellect and will? Do you experience yourself as the temple of the Holy Spirit, being aware of God's holiness in you? Have there been times when the Spirit was *neither with you nor within you?*

Finally, come before the Holy Trinity and express your sentiments of gratitude and praise for when you responded to the promptings of God's Spirit in you, and sorrow for when you moved away from God and into desolation.

▲ *Reflection*

God's ways are truly ingenious. Jesus' sojourn on earth was brief. His public ministry lasted just three years, far too short a time to accomplish much by human standards, not to mention restoring and making new God's plan of salvation. No wonder it seemed to many individuals, including his disciples, that his life and mission was a dismal failure. In asking the Father to send us the Holy Spirit to become our next Emmanuel—God among us—and to dwell within us, Jesus ensured that his work would continue and be brought to completion.

Exercise Twenty-Three
MENTORED IN HOLINESS

▲ Scripture

"This much have I told you while I was still with you; the Paraclete, the Holy Spirit whom the Father will send in my name, will instruct you in everything, and remind you of all that I told you."
—John 14:25–26

▲ Summary

Jesus is our Teacher par excellence. His words and deeds manifest God's merciful love and passion for us, as well as reveal the Divinity's baffling mystery. His timeline of three years to bring about God's reign among us is short, far too short by human reckoning. He dispels any doubt and fear his disciples might have about the impending failure of his mission and life. Jesus assures them that at his behest the Father will send the Holy Spirit, who will be our Teacher and Mentor, praying continually in our hearts the prayer of humble gratitude and saving remembrance.

▲ Session

(20–30 minute duration)
You will be visiting with Jesus and his inner circle of disciples as he promises them the gift of the Holy Spirit who will teach and remind them of all the things he taught them. Ask the apostles to intercede for you so that you are properly disposed to receive the Holy Spirit as your Teacher.

You are seated with Jesus and his apostles. Jesus has brought you together before dawn. A small oil lamp is the only source of flickering light in the room. The warm glow of the luminescent lamp is comforting in the darkness and it sets the stage for a momentous promise that Jesus is about to make to you about the Holy Spirit. The mood in the group is somber. Jesus' public life is hurtling toward Jerusalem and crucifixion. Amidst questions, doubts, anxiety, and trust Jesus tells you that after he is gone the Holy

Spirit will be sent to be your Teacher and Mentor, to instruct and remind you of everything he has told you. In silence you ponder the promise Jesus has just made to you. Then you hear different disciples express their reactions to the announcement. What is your response? What feedback does Jesus give to them and to you?

Next, Jesus asks all of you to go away on your own to converse with the Holy Spirit about this momentous entrance into your lives. You invoke the Third Person and engage in a very personal dialogue. You discuss the following questions: *In what way has Jesus' teachings become more significant for you? What would you have to change so that the Holy Spirit could have free rein and truly mentor you? What are some of the blessings and graces you have already received from your Teacher and Mentor?*

Finally, all of you assemble in a circle around Jesus once again. Jesus asks you to share the outcome of your conversation with the Holy Spirit. What is it that you tell the assembled group of disciples?

▲ Reflection

Anyone who has had the benefits of a mentoring relationship knows what a valuable source of confidence and security the mentor provides. Gradually the student comes to know depths of self that could not have been fathomed without the mentor's help. There could even come a time in some relationships when the mentor's work has been done. The student has moved beyond any further help the mentor could offer. Receiving mentoring in the spiritual life is a very valuable asset and many saints, like Teresa of Avila, talk very approvingly of such a relationship. In the Holy Spirit, Jesus and the Father give us the best mentor and teacher we could have. The Holy Spirit brings to completion God's plan of salvation, revealing in us depths of holiness and love that we could never reach without the help of the Third Person. Indeed the Holy Spirit is our constant companion and friend.

Exercise Twenty-Four
TRANSCENDING ALL LIMITS

▲ Scripture

When the day of Pentecost came it found them gathered in one place. Suddenly from up in the sky there came a noise like a strong, driving wind which was heard all through the house where they were seated. Tongues as of fire appeared, which parted and came to rest on each of them. All were filled with the Holy Spirit. They began to express themselves in foreign tongues and make bold proclamation as the Spirit prompted them.

—Acts 2:1–4

▲ Summary

Jesus' Divinity broke forth through his humanity on different occasions. His miracles were signs of Godly power and divinity. At different times he forgave sins as only God can. He prepared three disciples for his passion and death through his transfiguration. However, his resurrection was the greatest sign that he was God. In similar fashion, the appearance within tongues of fire is the Holy Spirit's epiphany to the world. God's Holy Spirit is at work in us and among us to bring to completion God's plan of salvation, restored and made new in Jesus.

▲ Session

(20–30 minute duration)
In this session you are seeking the Holy Spirit's anointing and power. You are gathered with the disciples. There is anticipation in the room as you prepare to receive the Holy Spirit. Ask Jesus to prepare your heart to receive the free flow of His Spirit. Spend time alone with Jesus as you prepare for the Holy Spirit's advent into your heart. Go through three simple steps:

♦ *Acknowledge your sins before Jesus and receive his forgiveness.* Imagine you are prostrate before him like the publican in the Temple as you confess your sins. Go into some detail as a way of recognizing your need for salvation from Jesus. Specifically, what is the one sin that you need to confess?

◆ *Make a firm commitment to follow closely in Jesus' footsteps by following his commandments and teaching.* Go into some detail and be aware of any reservations you might still have about what Jesus asks of you. In prayer it is important that we address honestly whatever reservations or ambivalence we might experience toward answering Jesus' call to us.

◆ *Receive the Spirit of Truth, before whom there can be no lying or falsehood.* Do you really want to receive this Spirit of Truth and are you willing to adjust your life to this divine presence in your heart? Henceforth you can never be a person of the Lie. Seeking the umbrage of the Holy Spirit is electing to live in the Light.

Next, you are assembled with Mary, the Mother of Jesus, other women such as Mary Magdalene, and the eleven disciples. As a group you devote yourselves to glorifying and praising God, the source of all goodness and salvation. Suddenly, you become aware of the Holy Spirit's presence "among you and within you" (Jn 14:17). In silent gratitude you adore the Holy Spirit in you and express your gratitude to the Holy Trinity for the gift of the Spirit as your Counselor and Companion.

▲ *Reflection*

The feast of Pentecost celebrates the descent of the Holy Spirit upon the disciples and upon subsequent generations of Christian disciples. Pentecost heralds the era of the Church and the domain of the Holy Spirit. Over the centuries, the Spirit has been the Good Shepherd, leading God's people slowly and inexorably into the Holy of Holies, the Heart of God. This Advocate has empowered and shaped the Body of Christ among us. No evil power on earth or in the heavens can vanquish the power of the Spirit. In spite of tribulations, apparent setbacks and Church scandals, the foundations of God's Church, established by Jesus, are firmly anchored in the power and love of the Holy Spirit.

Exercise Twenty-Five
THE BRUISED REED RENDERED RESILIENT

▲ Scripture

This is the Jesus God has raised up, and we are his witnesses. Exalted at God's right hand, he first received the promised Holy Spirit from the Father, then poured this Spirit out on us. This is what you now see and hear.
—Acts 2:32–33

▲ Summary

When dealing with Jesus, wonders never cease and paradoxes never end. Jerusalem and Judea are abuzz with the destruction of Jesus. The promise of the future Messiah has receded into disillusionment and despair. The status quo has been restored. Life can proceed as it did. Jesus' resurrection shatters these stagnant mind-sets again. Empowered in the Spirit, Jesus has been raised from the dead. Empowered by the Spirit, Peter preaches and witnesses boldly about his risen Lord and Savior.

▲ Session

(20–30 minute duration)
As you prepare for prayer, remind yourself that with God everything is possible. With anticipation ask the Holy Spirit to irrigate your heart so that the fertile seed of God's promises and expectations bears fruit in you.

Several images thrust themselves out of the event on which you are going to pray:

♦ There is the mind-boggling and heart-throbbing event of Jesus' resurrection from the dead. Imagine you are in the tomb before the dead and mangled corpse of Jesus. Before your very eyes his body comes to transformed life. Radiance and glory emanate from his being. Peace and amazement envelop you. In receiving the Holy Spirit promised by the Father, Jesus is exalted at God's right hand, full of power and majesty. Jesus is God. You prostrate yourself in adoration and wonder before the risen Lord as the mystery subdues you into silence.

♦ Jesus tells you that he can't keep the Holy Spirit to himself. You are deeply moved by his joyous selflessness. Peace and security surround you. You are hushed as a weaned child on your mother's lap. Jesus then offers you the gift of the Holy Spirit whom you experience as being poured over and into you. You feel anointed and renewed. Once again you prostrate yourself in adoration before the risen Jesus. You adore the Holy Spirit in you as well. Henceforth "temple of the Holy Spirit" will be your identity.

♦ Peter tells his audience that the apostles are witnesses to the resurrection of Jesus. With their own eyes they have beheld their risen Lord. From him they have received the power and anointing of the Holy Spirit. The core of their beings has been re-created. They are now walking boldly in the footsteps of their Master and their behavior will pattern his. You are impressed with Peter's fearlessness, eloquence, and conviction as he witnesses to Jesus being the Messiah and Son of God. Jesus has made you his witness as well. In thanksgiving ask Jesus why he chose you and what he wants you to do for him.

▲ *Reflection*

On different occasions Jesus opened the window to his divinity and it became clear to his bystanders and witnesses that he was more than a mere mortal. His claims to being God were confirmed through these divine interventions into human affairs. In some instances the witnesses to his miracles were ecstatic and exuberant at what they experienced. In other instances they were subdued into reverence and adoration. God's mystery has been revealed to us through Jesus. The Holy Spirit will continue to reveal the depths of this divine Presence among us. It is enough that we are brought into the depths of God's mystery and nourished by it; there is no need to exhaust or comprehend it. Faith, not human understanding, is the pathway into God's heart.

Exercise Twenty-Six
REPENTANCE—ACCESS TO THE SPIRIT

▲ Scripture

Peter answered: "You must reform and be baptized, each one of you, in the name of Jesus Christ, that your sins may be forgiven; then you will receive the gift of the Holy Spirit. It was to you and your children that the promise was made, and to all those still far off whom the Lord our God calls."
—Acts 2:38–39

▲ Summary

Have you wondered why you have not experienced the power of the Holy Spirit, or lost those powerful stirrings you once had? According to Peter, repentance and forgiveness are the keys to the Holy Spirit's empowerment. Jesus becomes your Savior when you acknowledge your sins and seek his forgiveness. The Holy Spirit then becomes your Advocate and deepens this work of salvation, pointing you in God's direction. Jesus and the Holy Spirit are two distinct persons of the same Trinity. They work in tandem and as one with the Father. They share the same divine life and mission of bringing salvation to the whole world.

▲ Session

(20–30 minute duration)

You are about to enter God's holy space. Many, like Moses, Isaiah, and the apostles are transformed in this holy space. Ask the Holy Spirit to prepare you for whatever spiritual transformation God wishes for you.

Peter talks about four significant realities that are important facets of the divine life imparted to us. They are repentance, baptism, forgiveness of sins, and reception of the Holy Spirit.

♦ *Repentance:* Repentance is a twofold decision: moving away from sin and turning toward God. Repentance sets right your moral compass and follows from a personal and intimate relationship with Jesus. Before you commit to Jesus' commands and precepts, you commit to *Him*! Jesus makes it possible for you to walk in God's ways. Do you need to talk to Jesus regarding repentance? What does Jesus tell you?

♦ *Baptism:* Baptism made you a child of God, bestowing upon you in Jesus Christ every spiritual blessing in heaven. Ponder over the powerful symbolism of this sacrament: soiled by sin you are plunged into cleansing waters and emerge regenerated in the name of the Father, Son, and Holy Spirit. The sacramental anointing with oil symbolizes the reception of the Holy Spirit's power and guidance.

♦ *Forgiveness of sins:* How comfortable have you become in acknowledging your sins before God? What effort do you make to confess your sins before others when the occasion is appropriate? Have an honest dialogue with Jesus. Ask for the understanding that he can only be your Savior if you admit you are a sinner.

♦ *Reception of the Holy Spirit:* The apostles have received the Holy Spirit. They have experienced repentance and forgiveness of their sins. They are transformed and filled with the grace and power of God. Their listeners have the same potential, but the promise of new life has not yet been realized. See them repenting of their sins and being baptized and receiving the Holy Spirit. Now they have the same inexpressible joy and consolation of the apostles. Express your sentiments to Jesus as you witness the transformation.

▲ Reflection

What a sea change has occurred in Peter! From being an impulsive and frightened disciple who denied his Master three times, he has been transformed into a courageous and powerful witness. Jesus has indeed been vindicated in choosing him to be the head of his Church! What better example to understand the difference between the results of relying on human strength and on God's power! No earthly power can withstand the power and certainty of God's truth!

Exercise Twenty-Seven
THE COWARD MADE BOLD

▲ Scripture

Then Peter, filled with the Holy Spirit, spoke up: "Leaders of the people! Elders! If we must answer today for a good deed done to a cripple and explain how he was restored to health, then you and all the people of Israel must realize that it was done in the name of Jesus Christ the Nazorean whom you crucified and whom God raised from the dead. In the power of that name this man stands before you perfectly sound."

—Acts 4:8–10

▲ Summary

Once again God's power and divinity break forth through Jesus, shattering barriers and prejudices erected from greed and ambition as well as fear and insecurity. Peter says that Jesus will not be destroyed because God has raised him from the dead. His mission of saving the world continues. Peter has been empowered by the Holy Spirit. In Jesus' name he has cured the crippled man who now stands before them perfectly sound.

▲ Session

(20–30 minute duration)
Ask the Holy Spirit to give you a guileless and eager heart as you witness God's power and salvation in this miraculous event.

You are at the temple gate called "the Beautiful." Pilgrims and worshippers, beggars and merchants wend their way past you. A crippled man is brought in and placed near you. Crippled from birth, he is more than forty years old. He comes here daily to beg for his living. As you converse with each other, Peter and John pass by. Instinctively the lame man asks for a handout. Peter and John fix their gazes on him. Hoping to get something, the beggar gives them his whole attention. Peter says: "I have neither silver nor gold, but what I have I give you! In the name of Jesus Christ the

Nazorean, walk!" You are spellbound as you witness the scene. Peter pulls him up by his right hand. The beggar's feet and ankles immediately become strong. He jumps up, stands for a moment, and begins to walk around. You are witnessing a miracle. The healed man is exuberant with joy and gratitude. The onlookers recognize him and are stupefied with astonishment. They clearly echo your sentiments!

You experience Peter's self-assurance and joy as he witnesses about Jesus. Suddenly an angry group of priests, the captain of the temple guard, and the Sadducees surround Peter and John. They are upset because Peter is witnessing to Jesus' resurrection. They arrest Peter and John and throw them in jail for the night. The following morning the apostles witness before the Sanhedrin. Filled with the Holy Spirit, Peter witnesses boldly to Jesus' resurrection without regard for the consequences. The Sanhedrin are amazed at their self-assurance and realize that the speakers are uneducated men of no standing. Still they can find no way to punish Peter and John because of the people, all of whom are praising God for what has happened.

Finally, you spend time alone with the healed man as he shares his miracle and tells you of his deepened gratitude, trust, and surrender to Jesus. You listen to Peter and John talk to you about the change that has taken place in their lives after the resurrection of Jesus and the pouring of the Holy Spirit upon them. Then you come into Jesus' presence and let your heart pour out your sentiments in gratitude and adoration.

▲ Reflection

Miracles manifest God's presence and power. They are compelling signs for some, leading them to faith and surrender, and are stumbling blocks for others. For the latter, God's messenger needs to be discredited. For the disciple whose heart has been strengthened by God's unwavering fidelity and love, all of life is a constant miracle. God's bounty and generosity is manifested at every turn and is a constant source of joy. Indeed the miraculous is the daily context of life. Like Peter they are self-assured because they live in God's embrace.

Exercise Twenty-Eight
INSPIRITED AND INSPIRED

▲ Scripture

There [Paul] found some disciples to whom he put the question, "Did you receive the Holy Spirit when you became believers?" They answered, "We have not so much as heard that there is a Holy Spirit." "Well, how were you baptized?" he persisted. They replied, "With the baptism of John." Paul then explained, "John's baptism was a baptism of repentance. He used to tell the people about the one who would come after him in whom they were to believe—that is, Jesus." When they heard this, they were baptized in the name of the Lord Jesus. As Paul laid his hands on them, the Holy Spirit came down on them and they began to speak in tongues and to utter prophecies.

—Acts 19:1b–6

▲ Summary

Here is another manifestation of the Holy Spirit's power to transform. The first transformation takes place in Paul, who until recently was Saul, the persecutor of the followers of Jesus. He has been transformed beyond recognition by the Holy Spirit and has now become a passionate follower of Jesus Christ. He is now evangelizing and baptizing enthusiastically in the name of Jesus and by the power of the Holy Spirit. John's baptism is brought to completion. The disciples are baptized in the name of the Lord Jesus. The Holy Spirit comes upon them and they witness to God's power and presence.

▲ Session

(20–30 minute duration)
With childlike faith implore Jesus to infuse your life with a deep awareness and appreciation of the Holy Spirit's presence and power; ask that the Holy Spirit be a living force in your daily life.

Paul is faced with an interesting dilemma. He comes across disciples whose initiation has not been completed. Not only had they not received baptism in the name of Jesus, they had not even heard of or received the Holy Spirit. Perhaps you have met Christians who have had all the rites of initiation but do not yet have a personal relationship with Jesus, or a first hand experience of the Holy Spirit demonstrating God's power and providence in their lives. Do they live in your own home? Perhaps in your shoes? Here are some questions you could ponder with Jesus:

- Do I have a personal relationship with Jesus? Is my relationship growing or stagnant?

- Do I have a personal relationship with the Third Person of the Holy Trinity? What have I done to cultivate and deepen this relationship?

- How prominent is the Holy Trinity becoming in my everyday consciousness?

Spend time in a heart-to-heart conversation with the Holy Trinity, addressing them one by one. Express your gratitude for all the blessings and graces you have received from God, especially the grace of belonging to the divine family. Express your sorrow for not being true to God's gifts in your life and make a firm purpose to develop your personal relationship with each of them.

▲ Reflection

God's mystery is both profound and unfathomable. It has so many facets that are imponderable and overwhelming to the disciple. While these facets of God's mystery can never be understood, they can and do reveal God's truth in the depths of our being. Some of these facets are: Jesus becoming human, the Holy Spirit being given to us as our Advocate and Mentor, Three Persons in one God, anyone who acknowledges Jesus as Savior and Lord becomes God's very own son or daughter and shares in every spiritual blessing in God's kingdom. In accepting and believing these truths of God's mystery, our lives are transformed and ". . . the life I live now is not my own; Christ is living in me" (Gal 2:20).

Exercise Twenty-Nine
BY THEIR FRUITS YOU SHALL KNOW THEM

▲ Scripture

When self-indulgence is at work the results are obvious: fornication, gross indecency and sexual irresponsibility; idolatry and sorcery; feuds and wrangling, jealousy, bad temper and quarrels; disagreements, factions, envy; drunkenness, orgies and similar things. I warn you now, as I warned you before: those who behave like this will not inherit the kingdom of God. What the Spirit brings is very different: love, joy, peace, patience, kindness, goodness, trustfulness, gentleness and self-control. . . . You cannot belong to Christ Jesus unless you crucify all self-indulgent passions and desires.

—Galatians 5:19–24 (JB)

▲ Summary

Paul offers a sobering reflection on our lives as pilgrims journeying toward the Father. Salvation is a relationship that begins with a conversion moment when we surrender and accept Jesus as our Savior and Lord. From then on it is a daily, and sometimes second-by-second, commitment to Jesus amidst the trials and temptations of life. There are other spirits at work that strive to negate and even destroy the work of the Holy Spirit. As Christians we seek the Holy Spirit's constant guidance and empowerment to abide in God's saving presence.

▲ Session

(20–30 minute duration)
Those under the influence of the Holy Spirit exhibit certain fruits. Those under the sway of self-indulgence produce a different type of "fruit," and are headed toward destruction and will not inherit the kingdom of God. Paul is asking you to do an assessment of your life in the Holy Spirit.

Begin by reflecting on how you shunned the Holy Spirit when self-indulgence dominated your life:

- "I, the Lord, am your God. . . . You shall not have other gods besides me" (Ex 20:2–3).

- "If you bring your gift to the altar and there recall that your brother has anything against you, leave your gift at the altar, go first to be reconciled with your brother, and then come and offer your gift" (Mt 5:23–24).

- "Love your enemies, pray for your persecutors. This will prove that you are sons of your heavenly Father" (Mt 5:44–45).

- "You have been called to live in freedom—but not a freedom that gives free rein to the flesh. Out of love, place yourselves at one another's service" (Gal 5:13).

Now examine your life in light of the fruits of the Holy Spirit: love, joy, peace, patience, kindness, goodness, trustfulness, gentleness, and self-control:

- "You will live in my love if you keep my commandments, even as I have kept my Father's commandments, and live in his love" (Jn 15:10) .

- "I tell you, there will likewise be more joy in heaven over one repentant sinner than over ninety-nine righteous people who have no need to repent" (Lk 15:7).

- "'Peace' is my farewell to you, my peace is my gift to you; I do not give it to you as the world gives peace" (Jn 14:27).

- "Love is never rude, it is not self-seeking, it is not prone to anger; neither does it brood over injuries. Love does not rejoice in what is wrong but rejoices with the truth. There is no limit to love's forbearance, to its trust, its hope, its power to endure" (1 Cor 13:5–7).

▲ Reflection

Jesus tells us that the Holy Spirit will be God among us. This same Holy Spirit will also dwell within us, being our teacher, mentor, and advocate. God's Spirit will lead us into truth and life. May we be docile and malleable clay in the hands of that skilled potter, the Holy Spirit.

Exercise Thirty
MADE BOLD BY THE SPIRIT

▲ Scripture

When they had led them in and made them stand before the Sanhedrin, the high priest began the interrogation in this way: "We gave you strict orders not to teach about that name, yet you have filled Jerusalem with your teaching and are determined to make us responsible for that man's blood." To this, Peter and the apostles replied: "Better for us to obey God than men! The God of our fathers has raised up Jesus whom you put to death, hanging him on a tree. He whom God has exalted at his right hand as ruler and savior is to bring repentance to Israel and forgiveness of sins. We testify to this. So too does the Holy Spirit, whom God has given to those that obey him."

—Acts 5:27–32

▲ Summary

This event illustrates the essence of the Christian message. The weak are made strong in Jesus. The repentant sinner is forgiven and saved. Human principalities and powers are confounded by the power of God manifested through ordinary persons who have committed their lives to Jesus. God becomes the *only* priority of the disciple.

▲ Session

(20–30 minute duration)
There are several kernels of God's truth in this event that could give you much inspiration. Ask the Holy Spirit to give you a docile and willing heart to hear God's word. Then consider the following:

♦ "Through the hands of the apostles many signs and wonders occurred among the people. . . . More and more believers, men and women in great numbers, were continually added to the Lord" (Acts 5:12, 14). *Be a silent witness to God's healing power and saving action through the apostles!*

- "The high priest and all his supporters (that is, the party of the Sadducees), filled with jealousy, arrested the apostles and threw them into the public jail" (Acts 5:17–18). *What is at the heart of their jealousy and anger, and how are these emotions present in you as well?*

- "During the night, however, an angel of the Lord opened the gates of the jail, led them forth, and said, 'Go out now and take your place in the temple precincts and preach to the people all about this new life'" (Acts 5:19–21). *God's ways and will cannot and will not be constricted and bound by human strictures and selfishness (see Is 55:8–9). Would you choose God over tribulation and punishment?*

- "To this, Peter and the apostles replied: 'Better for us to obey God than men!'" (Acts 5:29). *Have you been called at times to be God's prophet? How have you answered?*

- "He whom God has exalted at his right hand as ruler and savior is to bring repentance to Israel and forgiveness of sins. We testify to this" (Acts 5:31-32a). *The apostles were speaking from personal experience. What is the experience of your witness?*

- "So too does the Holy Spirit, whom God has given to those that obey him" (Acts 5:32b). *Peter holds that the Holy Spirit also witnesses about Jesus. But only those who obey the Holy Spirit would understand this witness to Jesus' power and presence. What kind of presence does the Holy Spirit have in your life?*

Finally, it is time to be alone with Jesus and the Holy Spirit. Share with them the sentiments and questions that have arisen in you about your discipleship. Let them teach and instruct you.

▲ Reflection

The Sanhedrin finally accepted Gamaliel's advice: "If their purpose or activity is human in its origins, it will destroy itself. If, on the other hand, it comes from God, you will not be able to destroy them without fighting God himself" (Acts 5:38b–39a). Gamaliel, a Pharisee, expresses the standard for true discipleship. Whatever is Godly in origin will persist and stand the test of time.

CHAPTER GLEANINGS

▲ Through the Holy Spirit, the presence and essence of Jesus is formed and strengthened in us. The reign of God bears fruit and is made perfect through the inspiration and leadership of the Holy Spirit.

▲ In the Holy Spirit we are blessed with the best Mentor and Teacher we could have. The Holy Spirit brings to completion God's plan of salvation, revealing in us depths of holiness and love that we could never reach without the help of the Third Person. Indeed the Holy Spirit is our constant Companion and Friend.

▲ For the disciple whose heart has been strengthened by God's unwavering fidelity and love, all of life is a constant miracle. God's bounty and largesse is manifested at every turn and in every event. Indeed the miraculous is the daily context of life. Like Peter they are self-assured because they live in God's embrace.

▲ Salvation is a relationship that begins with a conversion moment, when we surrender and accept Jesus as our Savior and Lord. From then on it is a daily, and sometimes second-by-second, commitment to Jesus amidst the trials and temptations of life.

▲ Discernment is a gift and a task. It is a gift that the Holy Spirit will grant us if we ask assiduously for it. It is a task because the Holy Spirit desires our cooperation in making every effort to do God's will in our lives.

▲ Constant companionship with the Holy Spirit, during formal prayer and during the day's events, will create a discerning lifestyle in the disciple.

CHAPTER FOUR

God's Dream—
Standing by Jesus' Side

There are several characteristics of discipleship that Jesus and his disciples emphasize in the Christian scriptures. Through his public discourses and private conversations with his followers, Jesus identifies the characteristics he expects in his disciples. The disciples themselves, after years of loyal devotion to the Master's ways, reflect on their experiences and express in their own words what discipleship means.

True discipleship is all encompassing and impacts every aspect of life. Discipleship is an inspired mission of love and service for the benefit of the world. Let us look at some of the salient features of the lifestyle we now call discipleship.

CALLED BY JESUS

From the gospel accounts we know that Jesus chose twelve disciples to join him in his ministry and to continue his mission after his resurrection and ascension. He chose these men from all walks of life—fishermen, political activists, tax collectors. Nothing really distinguished them other than the fact that they were ordinary, common men who answered positively when Jesus called them. Matthew was a reviled tax collector and Simon was a former member of the Zealot Party. Judas, who held a position of trust, in the end turned traitor. These nondescript men spent three years with Jesus being taught and gradually shaped to walk in his footsteps.

QUESTIONABLE CREDENTIALS

The apostles had questionable credentials by human standards. Peter, Andrew, James, and John were uneducated fishermen, yet all of them were leaders of the early Church, especially Peter. There were instances during Jesus' public ministry when Peter's example was both inspiring and impressive. After a number of Jesus' disciples were shocked and scandalized that Jesus spoke of himself as the bread that came down from heaven and the necessity of eating this bread, his body, to have eternal life, they refused to stay in his company. Despite the charged atmosphere in which everyone's faith was put to the test, Peter professed his confidence in Jesus: "Lord, to whom shall we go? You have the words of eternal life. We have come to believe; we are convinced that you are God's holy one" (Jn 6:68–69). Yet this same Peter, when the time came to show his mettle, denied his Master three times. And these denials occurred after he had made vehement protests that he would never betray his Lord.

Judas Iscariot began well. He was entrusted with the finances of the group. He even seemed zealous about the restoration of Israel to its political independence by Jesus serving as a political savior. In the end he betrayed his Master for thirty silver coins.

Nothing is known of the other Simon except that he was a disciple of Jesus and a former member of the Zealot Party. In the disciples' era, the Zealot Party was a recognized Jewish sect that represented the extreme of fanatic nationalism. They used violent means to gain their ends. Their belief in the messianism of the Hebrew scriptures was entirely limited to the recovery of Jewish independence. They believed in the worship of Yahweh alone and were adamant that acceptance of foreign domination and payment of taxes to a foreign ruler was a blasphemy against Yahweh.

Given that Simon was a former member of the Zealot Party, it must have been difficult for him to get along with Matthew, who was a former tax collector. In the gospels, "publicans (tax collectors) and sinners" form the usual pair. Publicans are also paired with gentiles. The moral character of the publican is alleged to be at the lowest level, just short of total dishonesty and corruption. The tax collector was an agent of the foreign imperial government of Rome, and thus worked against what his fellow citizens considered their welfare. Notwithstanding this civic image, publicans enjoyed a certain favor with Jesus. Not only was Matthew a publican, but he was called directly from the tax collector's table. In his favor, he did not hesitate to follow Jesus when he was called.

The sons of Zebedee were diamonds in the rough. Their mother asked that the brothers might sit next to Jesus in his kingdom, one on his right and the other on his left (Mt 20:20–21). John and James also asked Jesus whether they should call down fire from heaven to strike the inhospitable Samaritans (Lk 9:54). It was almost certainly on this account that Jesus nicknamed them Boanerges, "sons of thunder" (Mk 3:17).

Thomas is given unusual prominence in John's gospel. John 11:16 suggests a generous and impetuous temperament. He urges the other disciples to accompany Jesus into Judea and die with him, which is not what is suggested by the most famous incident regarding Thomas, the episode which has created the phrase "doubting Thomas" (Jn 20:24–29). In the final analysis, the lessons of discipleship that Thomas is taught by Christ are lessons each believer must learn.

FORMATION IN DISCIPLESHIP

Jesus spent three years molding this diverse group of individuals to carry on his mission of bringing God's reign into our world. Gradually they came to understand that Jesus was not only sent from God, but *was* God. This was a dramatic period of deepening faith and harrowing doubts, of elevated excitement and profound apprehension, of hope and despair. They witnessed miracles and began to comprehend that Jesus was no ordinary prophet.

During this time of formation, he gave his disciples special insight into his divine origins. He raised Lazarus from the dead and proclaimed himself to be "the resurrection and the life." He selected Peter, James, and John to accompany him to Mount Tabor and was transfigured before them. He laid claim to being the Son of God and he substantiated this through his miracles, the forgiveness of sins, and ultimately, his resurrection and ascension. He made predictions and promises, all of which came to fruition.

The relationship between Jesus and his disciples went beyond that of a rabbi and his followers. Jesus demanded a more complete personal surrender than did the rabbis of the synagogues. Jesus taught a comprehensive discipleship that called for a willingness to abandon everything in the pursuit of God's dream (Mt 10:37ff; Lk 14:26ff).

In his first letter, John accurately portrays the disciples as witnesses of Jesus' divine mission. He indicates that their authority and credibility come from being companions of Jesus, eating and drinking with him, knowing him at close quarters for an extended time. In his prologue, John describes the formation of these witnesses into disciples:

This is what we proclaim to you: what was from the beginning, what we have heard, what we have seen with our eyes, what we have looked upon and our hands have touched—we speak of the word of life. (This life became visible; we have seen and bear witness to it, and we proclaim to you the eternal life that was present to the Father and became visible to us.) What we have seen and heard we proclaim in turn to you so that you may share life with us. This fellowship of ours is with the Father and with his Son, Jesus Christ (1 Jn 1:1–3).

After Christ's ascension, another disciple who had never physically seen Jesus claimed authentic apostleship because he had been given an eyewitness experience of Jesus. Paul insisted that his calling was that of an apostle, having received his mission directly from Jesus. Paul states in his letter to the Galatians, ". . . The gospel I proclaimed to you is no mere human invention. I did not receive it from any man, nor was I schooled in it. It came by revelation from Jesus Christ" (Gal 1:11–12).

CONTINUED FORMATION UNDER THE HOLY SPIRIT

The transformation in the disciples solidifies with the resurrection of Jesus and the fulfillment of his promise that the Holy Spirit would descend upon them in power. After the resurrection Jesus demonstrated to the disciples that he was alive by appearing to them on several occasions in dramatic fashion. These firsthand experiences are important to the formation process of the apostles and serve to aid the formation of generations of disciples to follow in their steps.

The Holy Spirit comes to act as the indwelling counselor, bringing to completion the work of formation that

Jesus had begun. With the appearance of the Holy Spirit and the commissioning of the disciples begins the era of the universal church, the body of Christ. The Spirit was with the first disciples as they went about the business of establishing God's reign in seekers' hearts. The Holy Spirit is the herald of God's dream.

SOME HEARTENING CONCLUSIONS

There are some heartening conclusions that we can draw to enhance the formation of our own discipleship:

- ▲ True discipleship begins with *a personal call* from Jesus. Discipleship is not possible without a personal and intimate relationship with Jesus. A transformation takes place and in response the disciple makes a wholehearted commitment to love and serve the Master. The calling finds its release within this kind of union between Master and disciple.

- ▲ The call from Jesus is not based on any personal merit or noteworthy background. Race, culture, occupation, or language are not qualifiers when it comes to being selected by Jesus. The only criterion Jesus followed was to select those who desire to follow earnestly in his footsteps. Jesus showed that in every sincere seeker there lies the potential to live wholeheartedly and steadfastly the Master's image. In fact, a nondescript or disgraceful personal history seemed to receive greater notice from Jesus.

- ▲ Jesus' disciples were eyewitnesses rather than mere channels of a verbal tradition. They proclaimed Christ from their experience of seeing and listening to Jesus both before and after his death and resurrection. Present day disciples also experience the power and presence of the risen Lord, and ministry is a fervent expression of that experience.

- ▲ The present day disciple speaks of Jesus as someone in whose company they live all the time. His presence is transforming. Within this presence, the disciple is called and commissioned by Jesus as an ambassador to the world. Discipleship hinges on this identification with the Master.

Exercise Thirty-One
REST FOR THE SOUL

▲ Scripture

"Come to me, all you who are weary and find life burdensome, and I will refresh you. Take my yoke upon your shoulders and learn from me, for I am gentle and humble of heart. Your souls will find rest, for my yoke is easy and my burden light."
—Matthew 11:28–30

▲ Summary

Through the ages this passage has comforted and strengthened many disciples shouldering unbearable burdens. In these engaging words of reassurance, however, Jesus makes some quixotic assumptions. We are invited to approach him with our burdens, presumably to relieve the load. He continues by asserting that he will refresh us by substituting his yoke and burden for ours. We are told that his yoke is easy and his burden light. He concludes with the notion that our souls will find rest in bearing his burden and shouldering his yoke. What kind of burden and rest is Jesus talking about?

▲ Session

(20–30 minute duration)
Call upon the Holy Spirit to help you make sense of Jesus' words. Consider carefully this invitation to shoulder his yoke and carry his burden and in this way find true rest.

By this passage we can assume that there is a distinction between our burdens and his yoke. Our burdens choke our spirits and ravage our souls. Jesus' yoke is free from such wounding effects. With Jesus in your company, reflect on why your burdens are crushing and your spirit is heavy and suffocating. What does he suggest when he says he is humble and gentle of heart? Consider these thoughts in your seeking:

◆ My burdens result from wanting too much too soon. Real spiritual growth occurs gradually and involves a painful stripping away of our illusions. Such illusions are typically based on our human tendency to make somebody or something permanent that is essentially transitory.

◆ I am flawed, a sinner. One result of a sinful nature is that our faith is imperfect. As we grow toward a more perfected faith, we must deal with this tendency to "sideline" God in our daily affairs while foolishly assuming that we are in control.

◆ As I examine my spiritual pride, I can sense a consistent struggle in failing to understand that all I am and have is gift. Our giftedness is to be used for God's greater glory and not for every self-serving purpose.

◆ Continual surrender must be my lifestyle as a Christian. We often forget that death is present in every moment of life. In living the present moment, we must try to give God's will our full awareness.

◆ Jesus' burden is light and his yoke easy. As we walk in his embrace, we walk straight with shaky legs. When his teachings are allowed to find a home within, God's life pervades our soul and we experience true joy and peace. If we remain open to God's desires in every decision we make, our burden does become light. Our yoke is easy when we focus on doing and saying what is right rather than being reduced to ennui by trying to be tolerant of every position and whim.

Come before Jesus with your conclusions and reflections and engage in gratitude and petition as you ask for his blessing and grace on your discipleship.

▲ Reflection

If Jesus' burden is light, we never have to be like Atlas, weighed into the ground by life's burdens. Indeed, if Jesus' yoke is easy, an abiding sense of God being with us and in us will be an integral part of the disciple's consciousness. Given that our burdens—never God's—undeniably choke our spirits, when we are feeling weighed down we must look to see what of our own troubles we have added to Jesus' burden.

Exercise Thirty-Two
SAINT DISGUISED AS SINNER

▲ Scripture

Zacchaeus stood his ground and said to the Lord:
"I give half my belongings, Lord, to the poor. If I
have defrauded anyone in the least, I pay him back
fourfold."

—Luke 19:8

▲ Summary

One objective in a mature disciple's development is to distinguish illusion from reality. So often we accept illusion as reality, which results in our seeking God where God is not to be found. Zacchaeus was assumed to be a public sinner because he was a chief tax collector. This assumption fizzled before the reality of his discipleship. He gave away *half* his belongings to the poor! If by chance he had defrauded anyone in the least, he paid him back *fourfold*! Such behavior is the stuff of radical discipleship. Here is a good example of a saint being labeled a sinner, of truth being a victim of prejudice.

▲ Session

(20–30 minute duration)
In this session you are going to scrutinize your commitment to truth even when it hurts your self-image and ruins your best laid plans. Petition the Holy Spirit to help you with this scrutiny as you seek greater honesty and integrity.

Ponder the following statements that emphasize transparency and honesty. Dialogue with Jesus over each of these points:

♦ "Do not live in fear, little flock. It has pleased your Father to give you the kingdom. Sell what you have and give alms. Get purses for yourselves that do not wear out, a never-failing treasure with the Lord which no thief comes near nor any moth destroys. Wherever your treasure lies, there your heart will be" (Lk 12:32–34). *These words ring true of Zacchaeus. Do they describe you as well? Has Jesus become the reigning presence in your life, before whom every other treasure pales into a subordinate and secondary role? Does your heart truly rest in God at all times?*

♦ "Treat others the way you would have them treat you: this sums up the law and the prophets" (Mt 7:12). *Zacchaeus was not given this treatment by the bystanders, yet he continued to act from his heart. Are you more concerned with how others should treat you rather than with how you should be treating them? Is your discipleship tempered by the approval or disapproval of others?*

♦ "A sound tree cannot bear bad fruit any more than a decayed tree can bear good fruit. Every tree that does not bear good fruit is cut down and thrown into the fire" (Mt 7:18–19). *Are you a fruiting tree as Zacchaeus was, always in season? Or has your discipleship become barren and bereft of fruit?*

♦ "I am the light of the world. No follower of mine shall ever walk in darkness; no, he shall possess the light of life" (Jn 8:12). *As a follower of Jesus, are you walking in the light? What are the areas of darkness within you where you will not yet allow the light of Christ to shine?*

♦ "Today salvation has come to this house, for this is what it means to be a son of Abraham. The Son of Man has come to search out and save what was lost" (Lk 19:9–10). *If Jesus came to your home, would he pronounce salvation over you as he did over Zacchaeus? Like him, were you lost and have you now been found by Jesus?*

▲ Reflection

Zacchaeus displayed much courage and integrity. Though he was despised as a public sinner, in truth he was a committed seeker who sought Jesus as his Master and Teacher. Before he met Jesus, Zacchaeus had already begun to practice detachment and single-heartedness.

Exercise Thirty-Three
THROWN AMONG WOLVES

▲ Scripture

"What I am doing is sending you out like sheep among wolves. You must be clever as snakes and innocent as doves. Be on your guard with respect to others. They will hale you into court, they will flog you in their synagogues."

—Matthew 10:16–17

▲ Summary

In both Psalm 23 and John 10, sheep are described as weak and vulnerable. They survive and do well only when they have a good shepherd who ensures their safety and prosperity. Here Jesus is describing his disciples as sheep being sent among wolves. Is Jesus implying that the disciples will not be devoured because the good shepherd will be with them? In asking his disciples to be "clever as serpents and innocent as doves," is Jesus suggesting that in the world and in our hearts there reside the seeds of evil that will corrupt us if we do not seek the constant guidance and direction of the good shepherd?

▲ Session

(20–30 minute duration)
In your visit with Jesus you seek to understand the significance of his words. He has chosen you to be his disciple and to continue his work of salvation. Ask the Holy Spirit's guidance as you seek to understand Jesus.

♦ Jesus characterizes you as a sheep. He tells us that sheep will not follow a stranger, but will respond to the voice of their shepherd. Jesus has called you by name. *Do you recognize Jesus' voice and do you follow him? Do you really see yourself as a sheep whose Good Shepherd is Jesus? Have you followed strange gods? Or have you been scattered by thieves in the pasture?*

- Jesus says that you will be sent out among wolves. *Who are these wolves? Are they the capital sins of lust, anger, greed, pride, envy, gluttony, and sloth? To what extent are you a wolf unto yourself? And what are the wolfish influences in the community or marketplace for you?*

- Jesus says you must be clever as snakes and innocent as doves. *Have you arrived at a deep awareness of your capacity for deceit and deviousness? What does it mean to be "spiritually" shrewd? Do you have the innocence of a forgiven sinner, experiencing deep joy and trust as a result of being forgiven by Jesus and finding life by walking in the Master's footsteps?*

- Why does Jesus say "they will hale you into court, they will flog you in their synagogues"? Will you be pitted against the forces that oppose Jesus and all for which he stands? Many of these forces will have the veneer of respectability and religiosity. Witness the experiences of Peter and Paul in the Acts of the Apostles. *In following Jesus, do you understand and accept that you have burned your bridges to the ways of the world?*

Enter into a dialogue with Jesus about his call to you to be his disciple and a witness to his Name, and share with him the sentiments that have arisen in your heart.

▲ Reflection

Indeed we are like sheep, spiritually weak and vulnerable, sure to be ravaged by our own nefarious tendencies and led into harmful directions unless we cultivate the abiding and reassuring presence of the Good Shepherd in our lives. With the guidance of the Good Shepherd, "Even though I walk in the dark valley I fear no evil; for you are at my side with your rod and your staff that give me courage" (Ps 23:4).

Exercise Thirty-Four
SCARCITY AMIDST BOUNTY

▲ Scripture

Jesus continued his tour of all the towns and villages. He taught in their synagogues, he proclaimed the good news of God's reign, and he cured every sickness and disease. At the sight of the crowds, his heart was moved with pity. They were lying prostrate from exhaustion, like sheep without a shepherd. He said to his disciples: "The harvest is good but laborers are scarce. Beg the harvest master to send out laborers to gather his harvest."

—Matthew 9:35–38

▲ Summary

Jesus' assessment seems so contrary to our way of thinking. There is darkness and misery around him. The people are portrayed as "lying prostrate from exhaustion, like sheep without a shepherd." At the same time, Jesus comes up with an upbeat bottom line: the harvest is good indeed! He then makes the intriguing statement that laborers are scarce. Why such scarcity in the midst of bounty?

▲ Session

(20–30 minute duration)
In this session you are seeking the Holy Spirit's anointing and power. Greet Jesus as you seek to probe his mind and heart and understand his assessment of our world situation and what he wants of you in preparation for becoming a harvester in God's vineyard.

♦ Jesus' life and teachings are filled with paradox. He does not assess and draw conclusions based on convenience and conventional human logic. A shadowy situation can be a stepping-stone toward God. Salvation graces us when human endeavors have run aground. In human weakness, the power of God is made manifest (see 2 Cor 12:7–10). Thus paradoxically, "lying prostrate from exhaustion, like sheep without a shepherd" is a good situation, because it demands that we turn to God to transform our lives and acknowledge our powerlessness before the presence of evil. *To what extent has reliance on God through acknowledging your weakness and powerlessness become a way of life for you?*

♦ A sad fact of ministry is that many reapers don't really believe that they *themselves* are like sheep without a shepherd. They shepherd their flock with the mistaken notion that it is up to them and their hard work to "save" their sheep. Jesus seems to suggest that there are very few laborers who indeed rely totally on him to be the Good Shepherd of the flock and the minister's life. He further specifies that ministry is God's work of salvation in people's hearts and not the minister's! *Are you engaged in ministry that furthers your own kingdom, or is God's reign truly the priority in all your endeavors?*

♦ By asking us to pray for the Lord of the Harvest to send laborers into the harvest fields, Jesus seems to imply that if we pray with childlike faith and perseverance, the Lord of the Harvest will be moved to answer our prayer so that God's reign will be established. *Do you believe in the power of prayer? Can you see how the destiny of humans has been changed through it?*

▲ Reflection

It is so easy to forget that at all times in ministry we are ambassadors of the Lord, obliged to faithfully represent the wishes and intentions of the One who sends us. Ambassadors would be asked to resign if they chose to further their own agenda. When we do a good job of representing God's interests, the reign of God will flourish in human hearts.

Exercise Thirty-Five
CALLED FOR DEPARTURE

▲ Scripture

As he made his way along the Sea of Galilee, he observed Simon and his brother Andrew casting their nets into the sea; they were fishermen. Jesus said to them, "Come after me; I will make you fishers of men." They immediately abandoned their nets and became his followers. Proceeding a little farther along, he caught sight of James, Zebedee's son, and his brother John. They too were in their boat putting their nets in order. He summoned them on the spot. They abandoned their father Zebedee, who was in the boat with the hired men, and went off in his company.

—Mark 1:16–20

▲ Summary

Simon and Andrew, James and John have become role models of true discipleship. Jesus summoned them and they left everything to follow him. But did they really leave everything to follow Jesus? We know from subsequent events that the process of becoming a disciple and truly walking in the Master's footsteps was slow and painful. They had much to learn while adopting a radically different worldview. In time the Holy Spirit brought about the transformation that Jesus envisaged.

▲ Session

(20–30 minute duration)

As you prepare for prayer, ask the Holy Spirit to irrigate your heart so that the fertile seed of God's call to discipleship bears fruit in you.

Imagine you are in a boat on the Sea of Galilee with these first disciples. Take time to slowly ponder some of the startling truths that emerge from your conversation:

♦ These men were God-fearing and observant Jews. They offered no explanation for their "impulsive" obedience to Jesus other than the fact that his presence and call were magnetic and persuasive. Each one offers his first impressions of Jesus.

♦ Their formation in discipleship was a rude awakening. Each one of them talks about their "moments of truth" with Jesus, when they felt embarrassed about their worldly ambitions and shamed by their cowardice (Mk 10:35–45; Mt 14:28–33; Mk 14:66–72).

♦ They speak of the era of the Church after the resurrection of Jesus: their transformations by the power of God manifest within them and the workings of the Holy Spirit among the people. They tell of their newfound courage and fortitude in the midst of persecution and suffering (Acts 2:1–4; 3:1–10; 4:5–22; 12:1–19).

♦ They ask you about your own education in love with the Master and how you have been convicted by the Way, the Truth, and the Life. What do you tell them?

♦ Finally, you invite Jesus into the boat to be a part of this intimate visit. Each disciple says something special to you. What does Jesus say to you?

▲ Reflection

Patience, perseverance, and trust are essential to discipleship formation. Patience is crucial in acknowledging and accepting the huge chasm between our words and actions. Bridging that gap takes time. Perseverance proposes that we be prepared to begin anew day after day and to understand that the only real progress is to keep getting up after we have once again fallen. Trust gives us the peace and confidence to know that discipleship is God's work of transformation in us. We trust because God is true to the promises made to us as we step out in faith, willing to abandon everything in the pursuit of God's dream.

Exercise Thirty-Six
MISSION POSSIBLE

▲ Scripture

Jesus summoned the Twelve and began to send them out two by two, giving them authority over unclean spirits. He instructed them to take nothing on their journey but a walking stick—no food, no traveling bag, not a coin in the purses in their belts. They were, however, to wear sandals. "Do not bring a second tunic," he said, and added: "Whatever house you find yourself in, stay there until you leave the locality. If any place will not receive you or hear you, shake its dust from your feet in testimony against them as you leave." With that they went off, preaching the need of repentance. They expelled many demons, anointed the sick with oil, and worked many cures.

—Mark 6:7–13

▲ Summary

The twelve disciples are undergoing their formation at the hands of Jesus. He is putting them through the paces, giving them a foretaste of what their ministry will be like after he is gone. His instructions are direct and clear. They are to have no preoccupations with anything that would deter them from their mission, not even apparent essentials like food, clothing, and lodging. Their mission is to bring people to repentance by announcing the good news of God's reign through signs such as expelling demons, working cures, and anointing the sick with oil.

▲ Session

(20–30 minute duration)
Take a few minutes to prepare yourself for your visit with Jesus. You are about to enter God's holy space. Many humans like Moses, Isaiah, and the apostles were transformed in this holy space. Ask the Holy Spirit to prepare you for whatever spiritual transformation God wishes for you.

In this visit you are focusing on your formation as a disciple. Jesus has been working in you with good results. At the same time you have resisted his efforts. Consider the following scripture passages as you do an assessment of your discipleship with Jesus:

♦ "My being proclaims the greatness of the Lord, my spirit finds joy in God my savior. . . . God who is mighty has done great things for me . . ." (Lk 1:46, 49). *What are some of the milestones that you are aware of in your discipleship? How grateful have you been toward your Messiah?*

♦ "At the sight of this, Simon Peter fell at the knees of Jesus saying, 'Leave me, Lord. I am a sinful man.' For indeed, amazement at the catch they had made seized him and all his shipmates, as well as James and John, Zebedee's sons, who were partners with Simon" (Lk 5:8–10). *Peter was seized with unworthiness before the power and transcendence of Jesus. Has God's holiness subdued you into humility and adoration? It is a grace worth asking for, if you haven't yet received it.*

♦ "Whoever would save his life will lose it, and whoever loses his life for my sake will save it. What profit does he show who gains the whole world and destroys himself in the process?" (Lk 9:24–25). *There is no more compelling bottom line about the purpose of our lives than this one! Are your priorities directed toward making God the only true absolute of your life? What are you waiting for?*

♦ "Whoever puts his hand to the plow but keeps looking back is unfit for the reign of God" (Lk 9:62). *Are you becoming single minded in your devotion to and service of the Lord?*

▲ *Reflection*

When assessing our discipleship, we tend to focus on what Jesus is asking us to give up and how difficult each surrender is. Such an approach fails to recognize that discipleship is about receiving Jesus into our lives, about being transformed by his power and compassion, and about having Jesus as our Treasure so that everything else pales into secondary significance (see Lk 12:34).

Exercise Thirty-Seven

THE SOIL OF YOUR HEART

▲ Scripture

"A farmer went out to sow some seed. In the sowing, some fell on the footpath where it was walked on and the birds of the air ate it up. Some fell on rocky ground, sprouted up, then withered through lack of moisture. Some fell among briers, and the thorns growing up with it stifled it. But some fell on good soil, grew up, and yielded grain a hundredfold."

—Luke 8:5–8

▲ Summary

Jesus tells us that there are all kinds of disciples: lukewarm and tepid, eager but fainthearted, and generous and persevering. The lukewarm and tepid never do give God or themselves a chance. They are embroiled in the pettiness of their own lives. Their horizons are foggy. The eager but fainthearted start off well, but are soon discouraged by the vicissitudes and vagaries of life. They shrivel up in a haze of discouragement, confusion, and self-pity. The generous and perservering have the right balance between trust in God and willingness to do their part. They yield a hundred-fold whether they are aware of it or not!

▲ Session

(20–30 minute duration)
In your visit with Jesus, seek his assessment of your discipleship. Ask the Holy Spirit to give you a guileless and eager heart as you endeavor to answer Jesus' call to discipleship on a daily basis.

We can use the imagery of landscaping to appreciate the quality of our discipleship:

♦ Imagine you are putting in a new lawn or creating a new garden. Consider first the overwhelming prospect of all the labor involved: weeds, rocks, and roots. Perhaps pruning is needed. Possibly some trees need to be removed before all is ready! It will take hours of sweaty, dirty labor just to ready the ground for planting. You become faint-hearted at the daunting task that lies ahead. You convince yourself that your plants will survive, even in this poor soil, because they come from a good nursery, or because they will get plenty of water, or. . . . Without doing the hard work of pulling weeds and tilling the soil, you add peat moss and rich soil, and hope for good returns. You have a weedy future ahead of you! This is a picture of lukewarm and tepid discipleship!

♦ Now imagine instead that you have done the work needed for your plants to grow well. You weeded, pruned, dug out large rocks, and spent time turning the soil. Springtime wanes and your lawn and garden are doing well and are the topic of neighborhood conversations! Then there's a week of no rain, so you must do some watering. But hand watering is slow and very time-consuming. No rain for two weeks, and your resolve begins to weaken. You are losing interest in the project. Three weeks, four weeks, five weeks. . . . The grass is scorched, the weeds have taken root, and the flowers have wilted. You have so many things to do each day that you feel you *can't* spare some time daily to water your lawn and garden. If you're going to be an eager gardener, plenty of follow-through is needed! This is a good example of eager but fainthearted discipleship!

♦ Once more imagine that you've done the work of weeding, tilling, and planting. Your yard is your passion and priority. You have a deep, sincere commitment to the effort and spend time tending your garden daily, watering, or pruning, or weeding, whatever is necessary. You are to your lawn and garden what a shepherd is to his sheep. You will provide in *every circumstance*! As a result your garden produces freely and abundantly all summer long, thirtyfold, sixtyfold, and a hundredfold!

Converse with Jesus about the insights and conclusions you have drawn about your discipleship from these reflections.

▲ Reflection

You get out what you put in! Magnanimity and generosity go far beyond talent. They are the proverbial sweat equity. In the spiritual life, sweat equity is translated as dogged faith, unyielding perseverance, and abiding patience. This disposition is possible because Jesus has the same attitudes of dogged faith, unyielding perseverance, and abiding patience when working with us. Because of him we are empowered to become ardent disciples!

Exercise Thirty-Eight
UNCONDITIONAL DISCIPLESHIP

▲ Scripture

As they were making their way along, someone said to him, "I will be your follower wherever you go." Jesus said to him, "The foxes have lairs, the birds of the sky have nests, but the Son of Man has nowhere to lay his head." To another he said, "Come after me." The man replied, "Let me bury my father first." Jesus said to him, "Let the dead bury their dead; come away and proclaim the kingdom of God." Yet another said to him, "I will be your follower, Lord, but first let me take leave of my people at home." Jesus answered him, "Whoever puts his hand to the plow but keeps looking back is unfit for the reign of God."

—Luke 9:57–62

▲ Summary

Once again we are up against the challenges of discipleship. There is the treasure hidden in the field and the pearl that can only be ours at great price. We are looking at the deepest union with God shrouded in detachment, simplicity, and apparent renunciation of deep-seated ties with family and friends. Jesus asks for a radical commitment to God's will for us. Who, after all, is Jesus and is it possible to understand and live by his message? By his own admission what is impossible for humans is possible for God to accomplish in us.

▲ Session

(20–30 minute duration)
With childlike faith implore Jesus to give you his mind and heart, so that his teaching might make sense and give you a deep infusion of new life in him.

In this visit with Jesus you are seeking to explore his worldview and make sense of his sayings that seem so harsh and radical. As a way of helping you understand him, consider the following persons with whose stories you are familiar:

◆ The Roman centurion requests Jesus to heal his servant. In recognizing Jesus' holiness, the centurion sees his own unworthiness and knows he is unfit to have Jesus come to his home. Yet he has the utmost confidence that Jesus will heal his servant (Lk 7:1–10). *Indeed, a true disciple! No wonder Jesus was amazed at the depth of the man's faith and healed his servant without entering his home.*

◆ Blind Bartimaeus has his sight restored by Jesus. Many people scolded him because he was making a nuisance of himself as he shouted repeatedly for Jesus to heal him. Jesus was impressed by the man's faith and healed him. We are told that when he received his sight he started to follow Jesus up the road (Mk 10:46–52). *The disciple responds to Jesus' radical invitation after his heart has been deeply stirred by the Master's compassion and love, to the point of no return!*

◆ The Canaanite woman, whose daughter is terribly troubled by a demon, is a Gentile, an outsider who is not entitled to Jesus' attention. Jesus treats her according to the established social and religious strictures of the time, and even seems to insult her (Mt 15:21–28). *Her faith in him is rock-solid. It is a trust that has grown from deep despair and suffering. She recognizes Jesus as her only refuge. Jesus is greatly impressed by her faith and satisfies her plea. Another instance of what it takes to be an ardent disciple!*

Discuss with Jesus his experiences with these three individuals and hear what he has to tell you about your own discipleship.

▲ Reflection

Saint Ignatius of Loyola tells us that there is no knowledge that fills and satisfies the soul like the intimate taste of the truth. Discipleship is a matter of the heart. When Jesus' compassion and love have moved you deeply, his sayings will start to take root in your heart.

Exercise Thirty-Nine
COMING TO BELIEVE

▲ Scripture

From this time on, many of his disciples broke away
and would not remain in his company any longer.
Jesus then said to the Twelve, "Do you want to leave
me too?" Simon Peter answered him, "Lord, to
whom shall we go? You have the words of eternal
life. We have come to believe; we are convinced that
you are God's holy one."

—John 6:66–69

▲ Summary

Many of Jesus' teachings are difficult to understand. In
many instances they are difficult to accept even when they
are understood. In his discourse on the Eucharist he tells
his audience that unless they eat his body and drink his
blood they will not have eternal life in them. Such a statement is shocking and preposterous to many in his audience, resulting in a large exodus. Simon Peter, on the other
hand, speaks on behalf of the Twelve: "We have come to
believe; we are convinced that you are God's holy one." Will
you accept Jesus' words even when they don't make human
sense to you?

▲ Session

(20–30 minute duration)
Take a few minutes to become quiet and compose yourself
for your visit with God by listening to the sounds around
you, those in the distance and the ones near you. Then ask
the Holy Spirit to prepare you for your visit with Jesus
where the two of you will explore the depths of his heart.

Visit with Jesus using the image that Saint Teresa of Avila
proposes: imagine Jesus gazing at you lovingly and humbly.
He is at your service. Ask him to explain to you the depths
of his heart and the message he gives in each one of these
vignettes:

◆ "Yes, God so loved the world that he gave his only Son, that whoever believes in him may not die but may have eternal life. God did not send the Son into the world to condemn the world, but that the world might be saved through him" (Jn 3:16–17). *God's passionate love for you is all consuming and inexhaustible. Jesus' crucifixion and death suggest the profound depths of God's desire that you share in the divine life. Express your sentiments of gratitude and awe to God as you come to a fuller appreciation of this plan of salvation!*

◆ "I am the good shepherd; the good shepherd lays down his life for the sheep. The hired hand—who is no shepherd nor owner of the sheep—catches sight of the wolf coming and runs away, leaving the sheep to be snatched and scattered by the wolf" (Jn 10:11–12). *Can you ever go astray if your eyes are focused on your shepherd and you follow after him? The shepherd's every promise has been fulfilled, throughout the entire scriptures, but rarely as expected: Abraham, Moses, Jesus' birth, the resurrection, the eucharist. Express your sentiments to Jesus.*

◆ "You address me as 'Teacher' and 'Lord,' and fittingly enough, for that is what I am. But if I washed your feet— I who am Teacher and Lord—then you must wash each other's feet" (Jn 13:13–14). *Can you ever plumb the depths of Jesus' servant leadership? Still, you will always be nourished by it!*

◆ "I am the vine, you are the branches. He who lives in me and I in him, will produce abundantly, for apart from me you can do nothing. A man who does not live in me is like a withered, rejected branch, picked up to be thrown in the fire and burnt" (Jn 15:5–6). *What do you have to tell Jesus about your connection with him? What have you come to believe regarding God's "pruning" skills?*

▲ *Reflection*

God is always faithful. God's promises will always be fulfilled because God is not a liar! The disciple recognizes the Master's voice and never strays from his sight. Prayer helps the disciple stay in constant communication with the Master.

Exercise Forty
LAID ACROSS THE SHOULDERS

▲ Scripture

"I am the good shepherd; the good shepherd lays down his life for the sheep. The hired hand—who is no shepherd nor owner of the sheep—catches sight of the wolf coming and runs away, leaving the sheep to be snatched and scattered by the wolf. That is because he works for pay; he has no concern for the sheep."

—John 10:11–13

▲ Summary

Jesus gives us a preeminent description of himself as the good shepherd who surrenders his life for his sheep. He does this on a daily basis, constantly, consistently and unwaveringly. No enemy has a chance before such a shepherd. In contrast, the hireling saves his own skin and allows the sheep to be scattered, stolen, or destroyed. Has Jesus become such a good shepherd to you? Or do you still dabble and vacillate between belonging to Jesus and following other hirelings and/or gods?

▲ Session

(20–30 minute duration)
Ask the Holy Spirit to enlighten your mind and strengthen your heart so that you might be able to belong wholeheartedly to Jesus' flock. Resolve to make him the only shepherd of your life. Recognize the voice that calls you by name. His call is to be obeyed!

Your focus is on two questions in your visit with Jesus. Do you recognize and respond to the voice of the Good Shepherd calling you by name? Or do you still prefer to follow after some other shepherd? The second question is this: Are you a good shepherd to others in your ministry and service? Here are some biblical images you can reflect on and make the basis of your conversation with Jesus:

♦ Read the Parable of the Good Samaritan in Luke 10:25–37. The Samaritan, on approaching the half-dead man, was moved to pity. He

> "dressed his wounds, pouring in oil and wine. He then hoisted him on his own beast and brought him to an inn, where he cared for him. The next day he took out two silver pieces and gave them to the innkeeper with the request, 'Look after him, and if there is any further expense I will repay you on my way back'" (Lk 10:34–35).

♦ *Has Jesus become the Good Samaritan for you? Are you becoming the Good Samaritan to others in your conversations, service, and thinking?*

♦ Read the Parable of the Prodigal Son in Luke 15:11–32. *Do you truly believe you are the prodigal son and has Jesus become the father to you? Are you growing in compassion toward others, leaving all judgment to God?*

♦ Read the account of the repentant criminal in Luke 23:39–43. Jesus' compassion and magnanimity are awesome and defy all human logic. True repentance does indeed open the door to God's heart. *Are you beginning to understand that good works are the result of experiencing salvation in Jesus? Do you realize that salvation based on meritorious deeds is a spirituality of misguided self-centeredness and unhealthy independence from God?*

▲ *Reflection*

Compassion and forgiveness are godly virtues. On countless occasions, both in word and in deed, Jesus demonstrated divine compassion that confounded the mind and stirred the heart. He asks us to do likewise. The only true measure of Christian discipleship is the ability to forgive, seventy times seven times in a single day!

CHAPTER GLEANINGS

▲ Jesus' disciples were eyewitnesses rather than mere channels of a verbal tradition. They proclaimed Jesus from the experience of seeing and listening to Jesus both before and after his death and resurrection. Present day disciples also experience the power and presence of the risen Lord, and ministry is a fervent expression of that experience.

▲ Jesus showed that in every sincere seeker there is the potential to live wholeheartedly and steadfastly in the Master's image. In fact, a nondescript or disgraceful personal history seems to receive greater notice from Jesus.

▲ If Jesus' burden is light, we never have to be like Atlas, weighed into the ground by life's burdens. Indeed, if Jesus' yoke is easy, an abiding sense of God being with us and in us will be an integral part of the disciple's consciousness. Given that it is our burdens—never God's—that undeniably choke our spirits, we would do well, whenever we are feeling weighed down, to consider what of our own troubles we have added to Jesus' burden.

▲ Zacchaeus displayed much courage and integrity. He was despised as a public sinner. In truth he was a committed seeker no matter what others thought of him. He sought Jesus as his Master and Teacher. Before he met Jesus, Zacchaeus had already begun to practice detachment and single-heartedness.

▲ A sad fact of ministry is that many reapers don't really believe that they *themselves* are like sheep without a shepherd. They shepherd their flock with the mistaken notion that it is up to them and their hard work to "save" their sheep.

▲ Patience, perseverance, and trust are essential to discipleship formation. Patience is crucial in acknowledging and accepting the huge chasm between our words and actions. Bridging that gap takes time. Perseverance proposes that we be prepared to begin anew day after day and to understand that the only real progress is to keep getting up after we have fallen. Trust gives us the peace and confidence to know that discipleship is God's work of transformation in us. We trust because God is true to the promises made to us when we step out in faith, willing to abandon everything in the pursuit of God's dream.

CHAPTER FIVE

God's Dream—
Praying for its Fulfillment

PRAYER AND THE PRESENCE OF GOD

There is one prevailing truth that pilots the disciple's life: the conviction that Jesus is the source of salvation and meaningful transformation. He alone is the foundation on which the Christian disciple's personal commitment and faith are fashioned. Such confidence in the power of Jesus and the workings of the Holy Spirit in the disciple's life and consciousness can only develop through the assiduous practice of prayer.

Through prayer, the mind and heart of Jesus are formed in the disciple. Without prayer the disciple is like parched land thirsting for water. Scripture suggests that without fervent prayer, disciples are like sheep without a shepherd, living in spiritual confusion and exhaustion. In prayer the follower comes face to face with the tender mercies, as well as the holiness, of God. In such a presence the sincere seeker has no alternative except to become transparent and authentic. At home in the presence of God's love and compassion, the transformed disciple is refocused, and fears and anxieties are seen in their true perspective.

PRAYER—A TIME OF INTIMACY

In the creative hands of the Holy Spirit, the disciple is brought to a renewed appreciation of prayer as an experience of recognizing God's presence. This holy presence becomes both nurturing and necessary for the seeker's existence. The disciple begins to appreciate God's intimate yearnings for the salvation of the world and begins to sense that he or she has a special place in God's heart. A reading of Ephesians 1:7–9 provides an inkling of God's dynamic love for us: "It is in Christ and through his blood that we have been redeemed and our sins forgiven, so immeasurably generous is God's favor to us. God has given us the wisdom to understand fully the mystery. . . ."

It is incomprehensible to the human mind that God would desire holiness, blamelessness, and full love from each of us. Essentially these are qualities of the divine. Yet, through this grace, the disciple gradually learns to put on the mind and heart of Jesus. Slowly, realization of the transformation that is taking place gains momentum. There is progressive movement toward becoming holy, blameless, and full of love.

In prayer, as Jesus promised, the Holy Spirit reveals and puts meaning into the teachings that are recorded in scripture. Blessed with such revelation, the disciple experiences a peace and integrity that is not of this world. As the transformation progresses, the disciple journeys further into God's mystery and is privileged with wisdom and special insight about God.

Standing face to face with God's mystery, falsehood and hypocrisy begin to be exposed. Close proximity to the divine Presence can sometimes create a deep sense of sinfulness and unworthiness, similar to what Moses and Isaiah experienced. This same experience of humility carries through the writings of Christian mystics such as Teresa of Avila and St. John of the Cross. In this context, prayer becomes a place where one gets to know oneself as God knows us.

PRAYER—A SCHOOL OF FORMATION

The disciple understands the power of prayer and its ability to change one's destiny, bringing it in accord with God's desires. On numerous occasions Jesus alluded to the power of prayer and remarked that favor rested upon the petitioner who exhibits faith. In Mark 11:23–24, Jesus says,

> "I solemnly assure you, whoever says to this mountain, 'Be lifted up and thrown into the sea,' and has no inner doubts but believes that what he says will happen, shall have it done for him. I give you my word, if you are ready to believe that you will receive whatever you ask for in prayer, it shall be done for you."

True faith can only come with patience and perseverance, forgiveness of self and others, and efforts to abide with God's help in God's will. As the disciple sits at the feet of the Master, prayer becomes a school of formation. Under the guidance of the Holy Spirit, the disciple's faith is cleansed of inner doubts and fears. The Holy Spirit begins to exhibit influence in the disciple's consciousness, and other spirits are not allowed to dominate and encumber the disciple's thoughts and actions.

PRAYER—REFUGE OF THE FAITHFUL

Prayer becomes a haven and refuge from the burdens of the day and the yoke of life. Every now and then, when we experience the rough edges of our lives, desperation and hopelessness may invade our space and being. For many, the outcome of such travails is despair. Living then becomes painful and unworkable. Yet the disciple is taught an alternative in the words of Jesus, "Come to me, all you who are weary and find life burdensome, and I will refresh you" (Mt 11:28).

The disciple learns to distinguish between the burdens that Jesus wants us to carry and the burdens that are creations of our own egoism and pride. In doing God's will we might well be expected to carry a burden on our shoulders, but Jesus promises us that he will help us carry that load. He tells us his burden gives rest to our souls because his yoke is easy and his burden light.

Prayer is the place where many of the faithful have moved mountains. We recall the stories of Hannah and her son Samuel, and of Abraham and Sarah and the birth of Isaac. In the Christian scriptures, we have the remarkable account of Zechariah and Elizabeth, parents of John the Baptizer. These biblical texts are stunning and moving examples of lives being changed and destinies transformed through the prayer of faithful followers. Elizabeth expresses the walk of faith profoundly, "In these days the Lord is acting on my behalf; he has seen fit to remove my reproach among men" (Lk 1:25). The disciple knows that God will indeed deliver as promised.

Similar disciples, holy women and men, walk in our midst today. In retreats and spiritual direction I witness the deep faith of parents who refuse to give up on their erring or recalcitrant children. Some of them have heard and accepted God's answer to their prayers and have come to an abiding sense of peace. Others continue to walk in faith, knowing that God is at their side even though they walk in the dark valley. In my own case, I have experienced the miraculous on various occasions when God nourished the substance of my crushed and bruised spirit. Hopefully I will not want signs in my walk, because all of life has become miraculous.

KNOWING GOD BEYOND OUR UNDERSTANDING

Saints like Teresa of Avila and John of the Cross tell us that a maturing disciple might receive the invitation to enter into God's mystery in ways that seem baffling at times. Discursive prayer—prayer that uses human modes of communication like words, images, symbols, and gestures—may become progressively more difficult to achieve; it might even become unattainable. Consequently, the experience before God is one of distractions. Boredom, the apparent absence of God, the absence of consolation, and a prevailing sense of confusion are common symptoms inherent in this type of experience. For the ardent disciple, these changes can be frustrating and disconcerting.

This breakdown in the familiar manner of communicating with God is transitional in the spiritual development of the seeker. With time, and perhaps the assistance of a fellow believer, the disciple gradually appreciates that a quieter, yet clearer sense of God is beginning to emerge. In the apparent void, an ever-increasing desire to be lovingly attentive to God without the use of too many words or images takes root. The disciple's posture is one of listening. An advanced awareness arises that prayer is about God, not about oneself. Prayer concerns the God of consolations and not the consolations of God. Even in God's apparent absence, there is Presence. There is a renewed willingness to love and serve God on God's terms.

While progress may be unnervingly slow, the disciple begins to see that indeed much is happening during this quiet, inactive prayer. Changes are taking place in one's knowledge of God and commitment to Jesus and his teachings. Knowledge and wisdom are being given to the disciple. The Holy Spirit is praying within the disciple and true inner freedom to respond to God openly and completely is growing steadily. The Spirit is revitalizing the disciple's inner transparency.

PRAYERFUL LIVING

A hunger and yearning for God develops that a once-a-day visitation with the Master cannot satisfy. A need germinates to make Jesus a constant companion wherever the disciple goes. The Trinity is present with the disciple through life's daily tasks and hurdles. There is the distinct sense that the disciple is no longer alone in whatever transpires. Teresa of Avila believed that God is on the journey with the disciple.

At some point in this process, the disciple links up with some of the age-old traditions that have grown out of a similar process in the lives of countless holy men and women. The practice of the presence of God through the constant recitation of a prayer formula might become the disciple's way of keeping God in the heart and consciousness. Gradually there is a profound sense of the indwelling presence of God and the words of the formula are recited in the heart as an automatic response. Along with the formula, the disciple may well have the need to express sentiments of gratitude and intercession continually during the course of the day. And some will report that they are constantly conversing with God in their hearts, both talking and listening. Prayer has become an intimate reality in the disciple's life, as necessary to discipleship as breathing is to life.

Exercise Forty-One
UNVEILING GOD'S MYSTERY

▲ Scripture

At that moment Jesus rejoiced in the Holy Spirit and said: "I offer you praise, O Father, Lord of heaven and earth, because what you have hidden from the learned and the clever you have revealed to the merest children."

—Luke 10:21

▲ Summary

When all is said and done, prayer is God's work in us. We are the clay in the divine Potter's hands. Only God, solely at God's pleasure and discretion, can reveal the depths of the divine mystery in our hearts and lives. God's pleasure is not based on whim or fancy. It is fueled by God's deepest yearnings that we become his sons and daughters, holy, blameless, and full of love. Our participation in prayer clears the path for God's work to take place in us. As disciples, we understand the words of the Master that such revelation can only come to the "merest children," disciples who are weaned of anxiety, arrogance, and self-centeredness.

▲ Session

(20–30 minute duration)

Ask the Holy Spirit to deepen your joy and trust in the power and workings of God in your life. Then ponder on the truths that Jesus reveals in his response to the seventy-two disciples referred to in Luke 10. He is filled with joy through the Holy Spirit and expresses his praise and gratitude to the Father for the successful mission of his disciples:

♦ In joy and victory Jesus proclaims, "I watched Satan fall from the sky like lightning. See what I have done; I have given you power to tread on snakes and scorpions and all the forces of the enemy, and nothing shall ever injure you" (Lk 10:18–19). *What is your attitude when your spirit is burdened by the apparent triumph of evil in the world and many of your compassionate efforts fall on deaf ears and rocky soil? Does your prayer strengthen your faith and trust in Jesus' words?*

♦ "Nevertheless, do not rejoice so much in the fact that the devils are subject to you as that your names are inscribed in heaven" (Lk 10:20). *How strong is your realization that you have become a member of God's family and your name has been inscribed in heaven? Is your lifestyle commensurate with your heritage? Express your sentiments of amazement and gratitude!*

♦ "At that moment Jesus rejoiced in the Holy Spirit and said: 'I offer you praise, O Father, Lord of heaven and earth, because what you have hidden from the learned and the clever you have revealed to the merest children'" (Lk 10:21). *Do you allow the Holy Spirit to hold sway over you even in times of worry and confusion? This is evidence that you indeed believe in the words of Jesus. What do you still need to do to become like the merest of children?*

♦ "Yes, Father, you have graciously willed it so. Everything has been given over to me by my Father. No one knows the Son except the Father and no one knows the Father except the Son—and anyone to whom the Son wishes to reveal him" (Lk 10:22). *Does Jesus' assertion that he has control over everything give you comfort and trust in periods of pessimism and doubt? Has Jesus revealed the Father to you? Do you relate to God as to a very loving and totally committed parent?*

Take some time with Jesus and express the sentiments and yearnings that have welled up in your heart as you pondered his assertions that call us into God's dream.

▲ *Reflection*

The disciple's life is guided by the inspiration and guidance of the Holy Spirit. Vistas into God's mystery open up and understanding of God's loving designs for humankind grow appreciably. God utilizes the disciple's prayer as an umbilical cord to nourish us with life-giving power and wisdom.

Exercise Forty-Two
DISCIPLING THE LORD'S PRAYER

▲ Scripture

One day he was praying in a certain place. When he had finished, one of his disciples asked him, "Lord, teach us to pray, as John taught his disciples." He said to them, "When you pray, say: "Father, hallowed be your name, your kingdom come. Give us each day our daily bread. Forgive us our sins for we too forgive all who do us wrong; and subject us not to the trial."

—Luke 11:1–4

▲ Summary

Whenever we desire understanding about the dynamics and process of prayer, we resort to persons and books as our resources. When the disciples saw Jesus praying, they were both impressed and interested in learning how to pray. So they asked him directly to teach them how to pray. Maybe the moment has arrived for you to look to Jesus as your most important resource for prayer. Perhaps you can consider the following adage as your operating principle: when in doubt, seek Jesus out.

▲ Session

(20–30 minute duration)
During this session you will be entreating your Master to instruct you in his prayer. Imagine the Holy Spirit as a canopy over you as you learn from Jesus.

You behold Jesus giving you the prayer that he taught his disciples. Together the two of you ponder the significance of God's truth in each one of the petitions:

♦ *Father, hallowed be your name*—A relationship is always healthy and wholesome when we acknowledge the other person as he or she is. In our prayer Jesus asks us to acknowledge God's holiness, to understand that

God is totally other than who we are or think God is. Keeping this awareness of God will lead to reverence and humility on our part.

♦ *Your kingdom come*—The purpose of our lives is to praise and serve God. Therein lies our peace and happiness. Any other purpose would thwart our identity as God's image and likeness. Jesus is asking us to implore the Father to set our compass in God's direction.

♦ *Give us each day our daily bread*—Jesus asks us to preserve ourselves from the illusion that we are masters of our destiny, that we don't need God and can provide for ourselves. It takes true spiritual depth to keep such an illusion at bay and understand that we are totally dependent on our Maker every single moment of our lives.

♦ *Forgive us our sins for we too forgive all who do us wrong*—Since we are God's sons and daughters, God's nature is ours as well. Divine compassion and mercy are hallmarks of God's identity. God can only come to us when we live and operate within the parameters of our identity as God's children.

♦ *And subject us not to the trial*—Trials and tribulations will come our way. We will be tossed and thrown by them. Will we come out of them strengthened and purified, or swamped and crushed? Jesus tells us to ask God to give us the strength and faith to rely on God's guidance and power at all times, especially in our moments of greatest vulnerability.

▲ Reflection

Prayer is visitation and transformation. It is a time of rest and nourishment in God's embrace. In the presence of the Divine, the disciple gets in touch with his or her true self and can give recognition to their God-given potential. God's power and optimism are at work and transformation takes place.

Exercise Forty-Three
TREASURE IN EARTHEN VESSELS

▲ Scripture

This treasure we possess in earthen vessels to make it clear that its surpassing power comes from God and not from us. We are afflicted in every way possible, but we are not crushed; full of doubts, we never despair. We are persecuted but never abandoned; we are struck down but never destroyed. Continually we carry about in our bodies the dying of Jesus, so that in our bodies the life of Jesus may also be revealed.

—2 Corinthians 4:7–10

▲ Summary

For Paul, ministry and prayer went hand in hand. His life became a testimony for how they support and strengthen each other. Through this union, ministry becomes God's work carried out through us. The only reason we are worthy of this mission is because Jesus called us. Paul always kept this fact before him, especially in his darkest moments of being threatened, attacked, and even left for dead. He experienced God's power in the midst of his afflictions. The success in his ministry came from that same power of God being infused in him through prayer.

▲ Session

(20–30 minute duration)
As you walk in the footsteps of Paul, ask the Holy Spirit to give you the same wisdom that was imparted to the apostle. Paul expresses some of his deepest thoughts on the mystery of God's salvation while he experiences opposition from the community at Corinth. Let us reflect on some of his statements:

♦ "Because we possess this ministry through God's mercy, we do not give in to discouragement" (2 Cor 4:1). *Repeat several times: If God is with me, who can be against me?*

◆ "Rather, we repudiate shameful, underhanded practices. We do not resort to trickery or falsify the word of God. We proclaim the truth openly and commend ourselves to every man's conscience before God" (2 Cor 4:2). *Despite all opposition, do you believe, as Paul does, that Jesus will indeed triumph through you?*

◆ "It is not ourselves we preach but Christ Jesus as Lord, and ourselves as your servants for Jesus' sake" (2 Cor 4:5). *When this ideal of servant-leadership has become reality, the disciple is bathed in God's peace and joy. It is an ideal that the world considers foolishness and many disciples shun.*

◆ "For God, who said, 'Let light shine out of darkness,' has shone in our hearts, that we in turn might make known the glory of God shining on the face of Christ" (2 Cor 4:6). *Paul assumes you are not going to share with others what you do not possess. How deep are the roots of God's salvation in you? Have you become a light unto the world?*

◆ "This treasure we possess in earthen vessels, to make it clear that its surpassing power comes from God and not from us" (2 Cor 4:7). *Like Paul, are you continually aware of your powerlessness so that you are always dependent on God for everything?*

◆ "We are afflicted in every way possible, but we are not crushed; full of doubts, we never despair. We are persecuted but never abandoned; we are struck down but never destroyed" (2 Cor 4:8–9). *Paul is experiencing resurrection in the midst of passion and death. Is the core of your being undisturbed no matter what?*

▲ *Reflection*

Paul is a vivid demonstration of God's power and the triumph of the human spirit. He experiences the joy and victory of resurrection even while his thoughts are racked by doubt and despair. Buoyed by the strength and guidance of the Holy Spirit, the Apostle never wavers from metanoia, the path that leads towards God and away from sin. We would do well to adopt this unyielding commitment to God as a characteristic of our discipleship as well.

Exercise Forty-Four
PRAYER ON GOD'S TERMS

▲ Scripture

I have come in my Father's name, yet you do not accept me. But let someone come in his own name and him you will accept. How can people like you believe, when you accept praise from one another yet do not seek the glory that comes from the One [God]?

—John 5:43–44

▲ Summary

Jesus is the way, the truth, and the life. Accepting Jesus implies the embracing of all of his teaching and guidance. If Jesus is truly your Lord and Savior, there is no room for selective choosing where you and not Jesus become the yardstick of your life. No surprise then that many chose to reject him and follow their own way. Where are you in your acceptance of Jesus? Is it wholehearted and generous, or halfhearted and tepid? Your prayer rises or falls by this yardstick.

▲ Session

(20–30 minute duration)
Take some time to prepare for this visit by asking the Holy Spirit to give you a willingness to accept Jesus. Ask for a renewed passion to embrace the whole Jesus and all of his teaching, making his Way your Way, his Truth your Truth, his Life your Life.

Choose a comfortable place in nature where you and Jesus are alone. It is early dawn; silence reigns as the day begins to awaken. Your spirit is quiet and malleable. You sit face-to-face before Jesus as you seek to accept his invitation to wholehearted discipleship. To assist you, do a simple inventory:

♦ Fear and anxiety versus love—*What are the fears and anxieties that still invade your life? How can you be more trusting and loving? In what way are the objects of your fears greater than Jesus? What does Jesus tell you to do?*

♦ Guilt and shame versus forgiveness—*Have you forgiven yourself completely? Why will you not forgive yourself unconditionally? Have you forgiven others completely? Or is it the day-to-day forgiveness and acceptance that you find so difficult? What advice does Jesus give you?*

♦ Anger and resentment versus compassion—*Are you angry and upset about the way you have been treated in the past? About the way your life is unfolding in the present? Are you adamant about not judging others as Jesus asks you? Are you convinced that the path of compassion and mercy is the path of strength and endurance? What suggestions does Jesus offer you?*

♦ Pride versus humility—*Which are the specific teachings of Jesus that you do not yet accept? Name them one by one. Go against your resistance by asking Jesus to give you what he says is right and good for you. Pride or self-centeredness is the way of the world. Humility or God-centeredness is the Christian disciple's path.*

▲ Reflection

Prayer expands the disciple's spiritual consciousness. A path of prayer gradually leads the sincere seeker to accept Jesus on his terms, totally and wholeheartedly. A disciple becomes aware that faith does indeed move mountains when there is abiding trust in Jesus' promises. When we practice prayer on God's terms, we are brought into harmony with God's dream.

Exercise Forty-Five
PRAYER WITHOUT DEEDS RINGS HOLLOW

▲ Scripture

He who gives me glory is the Father, the very one you claim for your God, even though you do not know him. But I know him. Were I to say I do not know him, I would be no better than you—a liar! Yes, I know him well, and I keep his word.

—John 8:54b–55

▲ Summary

In this passage Jesus points out a glaring discrepancy in the spiritual life. He tells his audience that he and they claim to know the same God, yet a chasm separates their understanding and knowledge of God. Jesus gives us a simple and effective way to know if we have the true understanding and knowledge of God: if you know God you will keep God's word; if you keep God's word, you will know God.

▲ Session

(20–30 minute duration)
Knowing God is the work of the Holy Spirit in our hearts. As you prepare for your visit with Jesus, ask for the spirit of humility so that Jesus becomes your *only* truth and life. During this session go over your discipleship in the past decade.

Throughout this period you have walked steadfastly in the footsteps of the Master and have lived by the fruits of the spirit: love, joy, peace, patient endurance, kindness, generosity, faith, mildness, and chastity (see Gal 5:22–23).

Engage in a prayer of remembrance as you recall with gratitude the occasions and graces when you experienced the gifts of the Holy Spirit. Take each gift in turn and explore how you have experienced it. Appreciate the connection between knowing God and keeping God's word.

During this period you have also lived by spirits other than Jesus': lewd conduct, impurity, licentiousness, idolatry, sorcery, hostilities, bickering, jealousy, outbursts of rage, selfish rivalries, dissensions, factions, envy, drunkenness, orgies, and the like (see Gal 5:19–21).

When the Holy Spirit is relegated to the shelf, evil influences and forces dominate our lives. You become the hub of your life. Pleasure becomes your dominating behavioral code.

Recall with sorrow and remorse the many occasions when you chose other gods, when you thwarted the truth and lived a lie. Take each behavior and see how you have indulged in it. Once again, appreciate the connection between being in desolation and not demonstrating your love for God in deeds.

Spend some time with the Holy Spirit, your Mentor and Guide, and discuss your reflections and sentiments.

▲ *Reflection*

Love is a charade if words of affection and thanksgiving are not backed up by deeds. Similarly, prayer is a sheer multiplication of words if it does not lead to acts of devout service toward your neighbor. Ultimately, we know we believe in Jesus Christ when our profession of faith leads to "practicing what we preach." As James teaches in his letter, "So it is with the faith that does nothing in practice. It is thoroughly useless" (Jas 2:17).

Exercise Forty-Six
A HOLY HERITAGE

▲ Scripture

All who are led by the Spirit of God are sons of God. You did not receive a spirit of slavery leading you back into fear, but a spirit of adoption through which we cry out, "Abba!" (that is, "Father"). The Spirit himself gives witness with our spirit that we are children of God. But if we are children, we are heirs as well: heirs of God, heirs with Christ, if only we suffer with him so as to be glorified with him.

—Romans 8:14–17

▲ Summary

In this passage Paul lays down the context of our prayer. Prayer flows out of our identity as sons and daughters of God. We are God's family and our lives are lived within that identity and context. God is Abba, and Jesus is our Brother. We make our prayer while living with the loving support of the Trinity. As this life with God matures and deepens, we will know that the Holy Spirit is giving witness that we are children of God. We are heirs of God with Christ Jesus as a result of our spiritual heritage.

▲ Session

(20–30 minute duration)

As a member of God's family, it is always appropriate that we seek God in prayer as sons and daughters of the Most High. Ask the Holy Spirit to deepen your appreciation of your identity as you contemplate the major events of salvation history:

- ◆ "The Word became flesh and made his dwelling among us, and we have seen his glory: the glory of an only Son coming from the Father, filled with enduring love" (Jn 1:14). *Repeat these words several times. Adore and praise Jesus, your Savior and Redeemer. With gratitude tell him what he means to you and how he has changed your life.*

♦ "I am the good shepherd. I know my sheep and my sheep know me in the same way that the Father knows me and I know the Father; for these sheep I will give my life" (Jn 10:14–15). *Jesus says that he knows you in the same way that the Father and he know each other. In slow repetition of these words try to absorb the significance of Jesus' relationship with you. You will never plumb the depths of this statement, but your faith will be nourished and strengthened by it!*

♦ "I am the vine, you are the branches. He who lives in me and I in him will produce abundantly, for apart from me you can do nothing. A man who does not live in me is like a withered, rejected branch, picked up to be thrown in the fire and burnt" (Jn 15:5–6). *Repeat these words several times and express your sentiments to Jesus.*

♦ "I am the resurrection and the life: whoever believes in me, though he should die, will come to life; and whoever is alive and believes in me will never die" (Jn 11:25–26). *Through repetition relish the significance of these words.*

♦ It is in Christ and through his blood that we have been redeemed and our sins forgiven, so immeasurably generous is God's favor to us. God has given us the wisdom to understand fully the mystery, the plan he was pleased to decree in Christ, to be carried out in the fullness of time: namely, to bring all things in the heavens and on earth into one under Christ's headship" (Eph 1:7–10). *Has God's plan of salvation irrigated your spirit to the point that your consciousness is dominated by God's optimism and victory?*

▲ Reflection

For the disciple prayer is a precious and sacred time. It is precious because intimate conversation with God nourishes the soul and renews the spirit. It is sacred because the disciple realizes that life is about God and God's reign in the world. In prayer the Holy Spirit molds, shapes, transforms, empowers, guides, and teaches each disciple. Without this infusion of God's power both discipleship and ministry become a charade and mockery.

Exercise Forty-Seven
LIVING IN THE RESURRECTION

▲ Scripture

I continually thank my God for you because of the favor he has bestowed on you in Christ Jesus, in whom you have been richly endowed with every gift of speech and knowledge.
    —1 Corinthians 1:4–5

▲ Summary

The single most significant reality in the life of the Christian is the resurrection of Jesus. Every other dimension of the Christian mystery, including our own salvation, is subordinate to this foremost event. Paul is awestruck at the reality of Jesus Christ that includes our adoption as sons and daughters of God. No wonder Paul is filled with continual gratitude. With such an attitude, even the most desperate situations in our lives are tempered and put into perspective.

▲ Session

(20–30 minute duration)
Jesus' resurrection is at the very heart of your discipleship. It makes sense to continually immerse yourself in this saving event, to saturate your consciousness with the joy and victory of the risen Lord. This is particularly relevant in desperate and difficult circumstances. Ask Jesus to grace you with the gift of an apparition experience through this visit.

The empty tomb seems like an ideal place to visit with the risen Lord. Dawn is hovering over you as you approach the tomb to pay your respects to Jesus. You are both amazed and frightened as you notice that the big stone has been rolled away from the entrance. Tentatively you enter the tomb. In astonishment you acknowledge that Jesus' body is not there. While still in a state of wonderment, Jesus appears to you as a transformed person. You collapse to the ground in adoration before your risen Lord and Savior. Then Jesus lifts you by the hand and talks to you as Master to disciple, Shepherd to sheep, Sibling to sibling. You experience a warm, permeating Presence within and around you as Jesus highlights some fundamental realities of your discipleship. You savor the consoling realities he shares with you:

♦ I have overcome sin and Satan. Through my life, death, and resurrection, God's plan of salvation has been fulfilled. You are now my brother or sister and have been endowed with every heavenly blessing.

♦ You never need to live in fear. I am your God and have rescued you through the sacrifice of my life. I am your Savior to the end. I love you more than you can ever fathom. You are very, very important to me. Remember this all the days of your life.

♦ I have called you by name and made you my disciple. I want you to walk in my footsteps and represent me before every person. Like me you will endure tribulations, but fear not. I am with you always.

♦ I have gifted you with the Holy Spirit to be your Counselor and Mentor. He dwells within you and will reveal all that I have asked the Father for you. So stay close and consult the Holy Spirit at all times.

It is now your turn to respond to your Shepherd, Master, and Sibling. You do so in gesture, word, and silence. What gesture would most appropriately express your sentiments? What words would capture your experience? What does your heart reveal as you sit/kneel/prostrate in silence before your risen Lord?

▲ Reflection

Living in the resurrection spirit is both challenging and uplifting. It is challenging because when we are truly convinced of the resurrection and triumph of Jesus Christ, we must admit that our fears and preoccupations have only a secondary significance. It is uplifting because the disciple's spirit need never be intimidated or destroyed, since Jesus Christ is Lord. Continual remembrance of the reality of Jesus' resurrection is an essential dimension of the disciple's prayer.

Exercise Forty-Eight
ASSIDUOUS PRAYER

▲ *Scripture*

At every opportunity pray in the Spirit, using prayers and petitions of every sort. Pray constantly and attentively for all in the holy company. Pray for me that God may put his word on my lips, that I may courageously make known the mystery of the gospel—that mystery for which I am an ambassador in chains. Pray that I may have courage to proclaim it as I ought.

—Ephesians 6:18–20

▲ *Summary*

In making us sons and daughters, the living God has desired our cooperation and initiative in helping with the establishment of God's reign in people's hearts. Paul, along with other holy men and women through the ages, believes that our prayers can and do unlock the treasures of God's compassion and love as well as break down the resistances in people's hearts toward the Good News. John is of the same opinion when he asks us to pray for sinners (see 1 Jn 5:16–17). Paul asks that his ministry be accompanied by the intercession of the church at Ephesus.

▲ *Session*

(20–30 minute duration)
Take some time asking the Holy Spirit to prepare you for this visit with God and to give you a deep conviction of the power of intercession before the throne of God.

There is something mysterious about the prayer of intercession. Jesus has given us a power before God that seems incomprehensible. In John 15 Jesus states that saints have the ability before God to change the destiny of humans. While we may never be able to completely comprehend Jesus' teaching, we can trust his promise and intercede for the world. Let us consider the way you intercede before God and whether you comply with the prerequisites Jesus requires:

♦ *Faith*—Jesus required faith of anyone who asked him for a miracle or favor (refer to Mk 9:14–29 and 11:23–24). When you pray, do you really believe that Jesus will grant your request?

♦ *Perseverance*—Jesus asked us to persevere in our requests (refer to Luke 11:5–13). Perseverance will tell us whether we are serious about our prayer requests. Perseverance can also help strengthen our faith, especially when it is shaky.

♦ *Forgiveness*—The Lord's Prayer is a prayer of intercession. At the end of the prayer, Jesus says, "If you forgive the faults of others, your heavenly Father will forgive you yours. If you do not forgive others, neither will your Father forgive you" (refer to Mt 6:14–15 and Mk 11:25). Loss of love in our hearts leads to loss of union with God. Your empowerment dwindles.

♦ *Alliance with Jesus*—This disposition is referred to in John 15: "If you live in me, and my words stay part of you, you may ask what you will—it will be done for you" (Jn 15:7). God will not resist a loving and faith-filled disciple.

Spend time with Jesus reflecting on the way you intercede with God, and ask for the changes that need to take place in your heart and your understanding of intercession.

▲ Reflection

In John 15, Jesus tells us that if we lived in him and his words became a part of our lives, we could ask him whatever we wanted and it would be done for us. Such a promise becomes reality in the disciple's life when the Holy Spirit has transformed the heart and mind of the disciple. Through such transformation the disciple becomes one with the spirit of Jesus. The disciple's prayer becomes the continuation of the reign of God both in his or her heart and the heart of the world.

Exercise Forty-Nine
BURSTING WITH GRATITUDE

▲ Scripture

It is good to give thanks to the LORD,

to sing praise to your name, Most High,
To proclaim your kindness at dawn
and your faithfulness throughout the night,
With ten-stringed instrument and lyre,
with melody upon the harp.
For you make me glad, O LORD, by your deeds;
at the works of your hands I rejoice.

—Psalm 92:2–5

▲ Summary

Gratitude is an essential characteristic of a holy person. The seasoned disciple has become God-centered. The circumstances of his or her life matter only in so far as they relate to their devotion and service of God. God's reality has invaded their spiritual environs and physical space to the point where they are agog with amazement and astonished into awe. Gratitude overflows into their everyday life and circumstances. They can neither contain nor hide the joy in their hearts, a joy they can only express through continual gratitude.

▲ Session

(20–30 minute duration)
Spend a few minutes getting ready for your visit with the God of everlasting mercies and bountiful love. The context of your prayer is one of great intimacy as you remember that you have been made God's child through Jesus Christ. You beseech the Holy Spirit to develop within you a deeply grateful heart that is full of abiding thanksgiving for God's largesse and generosity.

Return to a scene in nature where inspiring wonder astounds you. My personal favorites are Yellowstone Park, Northern Ontario in Canada, the Upper Peninsula of

Michigan, and the Canadian Rockies. In this scene of brute splendor and sweeping grandeur, stand in breathtaking adoration before your Creator and God for all that your eyes and ears behold. Then focus on yourself as God's handiwork: the gift of life, your faculties, and God's constant providence in your life.

Next, see yourself at the foot of the cross, as Jesus is in the throes of death. He looks at you with great tenderness, shortly after promising the repentant criminal that he would enter heaven that very day. He tells you that he has suffered and is dying gladly for your sake so that you might share in his life and God's family. In word, gesture, and silence you thank him for his gift of salvation and divine life. In particular you thank him for his forgiveness and the decision to make you a new creation.

Finally, you stand before the risen Christ who has overcome sin and death. He lays his hand on your shoulder and sends you forth into the world, to bring the glad tidings of salvation and divine fellowship through him. You prostrate yourself before your Lord and thank him for giving you this extraordinary privilege, to walk in his footsteps and become his ambassador. You also ask him to bless and strengthen your discipleship and ministry as you go on your way.

▲ Reflection

A grateful disciple is a joyful follower. It is difficult to harbor fermenting resentments and brooding suspicions when one's heart is suffused with gratitude. A grateful heart is a giving heart. When gratitude becomes second nature, we are able to rejoice in the good fortune of others, without envy or jealousy. Even when difficulties swamp us, we find reasons to be grateful. In the ultimate analysis, if God is with us who can be against us? A grateful disciple knows all is well no matter what.

Exercise Fifty
LIFE SEASONED WITH PRAYER

▲ Scripture

And they complained to Moses, "Were there no burial places in Egypt that you had to bring us out here
to die in the desert? Why did you do this to us? Why
did you bring us out of Egypt? Did we not tell you
this in Egypt, when we said, 'Leave us alone. Let us
serve the Egyptians'? Far better for us to be the
slaves of the Egyptians than to die in the desert."
But Moses answered the people, "Fear not! Stand
your ground, and you will see the victory the LORD
will win for you today. These Egyptians whom you
see today you will never see again. The LORD himself
will fight for you; you have only to keep still."

—Exodus 14:11–14

▲ Summary

The disciple understands that his or her life has been given
over to Jesus. A covenant relationship has been established
between Master and disciple. Prayer has become the
essence of the relationship. Prayer can no longer be a mere
exercise or activity engaged in once or twice a day. It is constant activity reflecting the covenantal relationship. It pervades the disciple's consciousness in waking and sleeping
hours. Jesus is the disciple's Alpha and Omega.

▲ Session

(20–30 minute duration)
During this prayer session you will ask the Holy Spirit for
the gift of contemplation, even in action. This will enable
you to bring the Jesus you experience when you sit alone at
the feet of Master to your daily activities. Take a few minutes to quiet yourself through the awareness of your
breathing. Then beseech the Holy Spirit to help you be lovingly attentive to God's presence and open to whatever ini-
tiatives God may have for you.

Spend some time going over the various activities and circumstances of your life in the past week. Try to be as detailed and specific as you can. What went on within you as you fretted about the day and postponed, succeeded, or failed in fulfilling your plans and obligations? How prominent was God's presence in your consciousness during these events and circumstances? What description would you give to your interactions with others? Would you say you prayed only on occasion, prayed frequently, or prayed continually? Did you express abundant gratitude as well as ask for help in difficult situations? Did you experience God's consolations and intimate presence?

Now go over the same week and make Jesus present in every circumstance. Try to experience the whole week doing everything along with Jesus in praise, gratitude, and intercession. During your transitions from one activity to another, engage in repeating a short prayer formula that has become your anchor-prayer. Note the difference between doing it alone or half-heartedly on the one hand, and with Jesus and with full attention on the other. Closely examine the differing quality of each experience.

Finally, spend time making a prayer of renewed commitment to Jesus as your Lord and Master. Offer him your mind, memory, imagination, will, sense faculties, liberty, dreams, plans, in fact your entire being. Ask Jesus to help you become aware of his constant presence with you as your Good Shepherd. Ask for the gift of staying close to him at all times so that he truly becomes the essence and cornerstone of your life and ministry.

▲ Reflection

For the disciple it is not enough to visit with Jesus in Church or in a home sanctuary. The disciple needs to worship and commune continually and thus carries Jesus in his or her heart. Jesus goes wherever the disciple goes, into every activity, interaction, and mission. Jesus is the disciple's itinerant Teacher and Master. The school of love never lets out. It is always in session because the disciple needs continual formation.

CHAPTER GLEANINGS

▲ The disciple learns to distinguish between the burdens that Jesus wants us to carry and the burdens that are creations of our own egoism and pride.

▲ An advanced awareness arises that prayer is about God, not about oneself. Prayer concerns the God of consolations and not the consolations of God. There is a renewed willingness to love and serve God on God's terms.

▲ Love is a charade if words of affection and thanksgiving are not backed up by deeds. Similarly, prayer is a sheer multiplication of words if it does not lead to acts of devout service toward your neighbor. Ultimately, we know we believe in Jesus Christ when our profession of faith leads to "practicing what we preach."

▲ Jesus' resurrection is at the very heart of our discipleship. It makes sense to continually immerse ourselves in this saving event to saturate our consciousness with the joy and victory of the risen Lord. This is particularly relevant in desperate and difficult circumstances.

▲ There is something mysterious about the prayer of intercession. Jesus has given us a power before God that seems incomprehensible. In John 15 Jesus states that saints have the ability before God to change the destiny of humans. While we may never be able to completely comprehend Jesus' teaching, we can trust Jesus' promise and intercede for the world.

▲ It is difficult to harbor fermenting resentments and brooding suspicions when one's heart is suffused with gratitude. When gratitude has become second nature, we are able to rejoice in the good fortune of others, without envy or jealousy. Even when difficulties swamp us, we find reasons to be grateful.

CHAPTER SIX

God's Dream—
Reflecting Jesus Day by Day

In prayer and solitude the disciple imbibes God's yearnings for humankind. The intimate desire for our salvation and union with the Divine is generated in this solitude. Prayer is the place where the Holy Spirit mentors the disciple, bringing about understanding of God's designs for self and the salvation of the world. Gradually the disciple experiences a transformation in mind and heart and begins to put on the mind and heart of Jesus.

As the disciple is led deeper into the mystery of God's love, there is a profound sense of the limitation of the human mind and its incapacity to comprehend God's holiness and goodness. So disciples ask rhetorical questions for which they seek no answers. The questions attempt to delineate dimly the depths of the impact the Holy Spirit has made on their beings. Why would God, out of pure love, choose to share intimately with us the divine love and Spirit? Why would God never give up on us and choose to allow Jesus to become incarnate? Why would Jesus go to such extreme lengths to demonstrate God's love for us?

As much as the mind is befuddled by this indescribable profundity, the heart is moved toward transformation and faith deepens. The disciple is in the presence of inexpressible mystery. Silent awe and adoration seem to be the natural response, unless God chooses to give words and expression to the experience. An overwhelming sense of gratitude and humility permeates this reverence. The seeker is confronted with the remarkable reality that through Jesus, God would expect us to be " holy and blameless in his sight, to be full of love" (Eph 1:4).

The disciple's humility arises from the realization that so often he or she has thwarted God's desires. What gives the follower the confidence to believe it will be any different now that he or she has made this commitment to discipleship? In prayer the disciple receives the answer that what is impossible for humans is possible for God. In prayer the awareness grows that indeed God has begun a good work and is bringing it to completion.

THE DISCIPLE'S DEPENDENCE ON CHRIST

At the center of Christian discipleship is the seeker's experience of Jesus. Without Jesus the disciple's life and ministry are meaningless. Many followers enter into ministry with enthusiasm and fervor because their lives have been touched in dramatic and poignant ways, but, all too often, they quickly slip away from a solid reliance on their true source and sustenance, Jesus. They are the grains of wheat that fell by the wayside, or on rocky ground, or among thorn bushes.

The ardent follower develops the practice of depending on Jesus in every aspect of life. Imagine Jesus to be your heart, beating consistently all the days of your life, without any respite, so that you might have life continuously and restfully. Jesus restores and renews divine lifeblood in us continuously, so that we might live God's life to the fullest! The gospels speak of the disciple as the branch that receives its sap and nourishment from Jesus, the vine. Apart from this vine, the branch is fit only to be cast into the fire. The disciple flourishes in his or her dependence on Christ.

The disciple produces abundantly in ministry because "he lives in me and I in him" (Jn 15:5). Apart from Jesus, the disciple experiences an awareness of being like a withered branch picked up to be thrown in the fire and burned. Abiding and constant union with Jesus brings about a profound change in the disciple's lifestyle. Knowing how central this union with Jesus is, the disciple has spent countless hours sitting at the feet of the Master. Within this hunger to be mentored by Jesus are sown the seeds of conviction, that Jesus indeed is the source of the disciple's life and ministry.

AUTHENTIC ACCOUNTABILITY

The disciple has made it a practice to live conjointly with Jesus. Everything in the disciple's life is open to scrutiny and supervision by Jesus. Nothing is private or out of bounds in this relationship. The disciple does everything along with Jesus, for the disciple is no longer alone. Within this union of grace lies the disciple's true accountability.

Jesus always abides in and with the disciple. In a very real sense the disciple no longer has problems or challenges independently of Jesus. The disciple's challenges become Jesus' concerns. When faced with difficult or seemingly impossible circumstances, the disciple turns to Jesus for strength and inspiration, and together they meet the test. Sometimes the solution lies in bearing the cross together with love and patience. At other times the disciple moves forward on faith in the Master alone, without the advantage of clear sight, knowledge, or understanding.

PRUNING THE DEAD AND BARREN

Jesus tells us that the Father, who is the vine grower, prunes away every barren branch and trims clean the fruitful ones in order to increase the yield. Transformation requires the purging of everything in the disciple that is not of God. The disciple has come to appreciate this process of spiritual growth and urgently welcomes the need to remove anything that is not required in the advancement.

The desire to be free of one's roots of sin is generated by the disciple's experience of God's unwavering and overwhelming love for him or her. In response to the magnitude of this divine love, the disciple wants to reflect the Master in every facet of life. Like the holy men and women who have gone before, the disciple initiates a constant purification of any disorder and attachment that leads away from God. However, the disciple also knows that only trust and surrender into the arms of the Savior will bring this about. As the Psalmist so succinctly states, "Be still and know that I am God" (Ps 46:10 NRSV).

By sitting down in God's presence, at least daily, to examine one's consciousness of God during the day, the disciple slowly learns to appreciate the workings of the Spirit in his or her life. Through various movements, the Holy Spirit teaches the disciple wisdom and discernment, both to detect and avoid the occasions of sin as well as to encourage the movements and sentiments that lead one closer into God's heart. The examination of consciousness increases one's gratitude and repentance.

TRANSFORMATION IN THE POTTER'S HANDS

Ultimately, the adamant disciple sees his or her transformation into an image and likeness of Jesus through changes in behavior and attitude. As the disciple takes on the heart and mind of Christ, she or he is molded—reshaped—from mere clay into the pottery vessel that the Holy Spirit desires according to the divine purpose. This guidance enriches the disciple in every aspect of life, leading to experiences that are only possible by the grace of God. Let us look at several situations where what is impossible by human standards is made possible by God.

The Sermon on the Mount is replete with situations and teachings that are provocative, even offensive, to our human appetites and mores. Jesus' teaching on anger and resentment is a good case in point. He sets very high standards for his followers, asking us to love our enemies and pray for our persecutors. No longer is it acceptable for us to love only our family, friends, and countrymen. We are to extend compassion and love toward those whom we dislike and those who hate us. In fact, Jesus wants us to be as God is, forgiving and compassionate toward good and bad alike. In effect the disciple cannot consider anyone to be an enemy. A true follower of Jesus' New Way is summoned to treat everyone as God's very own.

How does such teaching become part and parcel of a disciple's lifestyle? Jesus knows that such transformation of attitude and behavior is not possible through human striving. So he asks us to rely on the power of the Holy Spirit to make us merciful and compassionate. The disciple takes to heart, and practices assiduously, the teaching given by Jesus in Matthew 18:21–22: "Then Peter came up and asked him, 'Lord, when my brother wrongs me, how often must I forgive him? Seven times?' 'No,' Jesus replied, 'not seven times; I say, seventy times seven times.'"

Whether we understand seventy times seven times to mean four hundred and ninety attempts to forgive each one of our enemies, or to be a call to forgive endlessly, such a formula brings about transformation because it contains within it a revolution. Whatever is not born of love in the disciple is brought under scrutiny and challenged by God's truth. Such scrutiny, when done with humility, integrity, and sincerity, engenders thoughts and actions that reflect God in every aspect of daily life.

A corollary of this precept to forgive our enemies and love our persecutors is to hold steadfastly to the command not to malign others through gossip and innuendo, even when what is talked about might be true. True discipleship offers everybody, friend and foe alike, the respect and reverence due to them as sons and daughters of God, regardless of their behavior. Jesus forgave his enemies from the cross and genuinely loved them, and he wants us to live our discipleship according to the same standard!

Another challenge to the disciple is to give God all honor and glory in every situation, and to take care not to sideline God and draw attention to oneself. The true disciple is taught by the Holy Spirit to see the illusion that lies in the pursuit of earthly glory and honor, and to recognize how easily we are drawn into good works for self-aggrandizement. Authentic discipleship appreciates that the path to humility leads through misunderstanding and rejection. However, when one has become truly humble, there are no feelings attached to rejection or disparity. Such a paradox can never be understood by efforts of the mind. It is known only in the heart where the Holy Spirit gives counsel.

Finally, one other transformation that the disciple experiences in lifestyle can be found in the area of material wealth and security. Early in our discipleship we cannot conceive that our attachments have become idols and that our wayward desires have robbed us of true worship. The disciple has made all the affairs of his or her life God's domain. The disciple is convinced that God will provide for every need as the birds of the air and the lilies in the field are provided for. Gradually the disciple learns to live in peace and sees that God is indeed providing for every need and more. There is an overwhelming sense of generosity and largesse in God's daily providence. Indeed, when Jesus has become the alpha and omega of the disciple's life, the presence and attitudes of Jesus become manifest in the disciple's lifestyle. The Potter forms and shapes the vessel out of which is poured God's dream.

Exercise Fifty-One
LONGING FOR GOD

▲ Scripture

Blest are they who hunger and thirst for holiness;
they shall have their fill. Blest are they who show
mercy; mercy shall be theirs. Blest are the single-
hearted for they shall see God.

—Matthew 5:6–8

▲ Summary

The beatitudes sum up all of Jesus' teachings. They are
stark in their simplicity and rich in their meaning. They are
paradigmatic statements, reaching into the depths of our
being and challenging every settled assumption we hold.
Throughout the beatitudes, Jesus extols the disciple who
has come to a willingness to go to any lengths to seek and
receive union with God.

▲ Session

(20–30 minute duration)
The beatitudes go against the grain of human nature and
society, and only God can make them attractive to our spirits. Ask the Holy Spirit to reveal the meaning of these beatitudes so that you might incorporate their spirit.

To understand these beatitudes we can use the image of
the Anawim, whose backs were bent double by the unjust
burdens they were forced to carry. In the spiritual life, this
image would translate as the tension the disciple invariably
experiences between desiring to follow Jesus and being burdened with a tendency to thwart such a yearning. This tension is resolved through prayer. As we come before God
with the realization that we are unable *on our own* to do
what Jesus asks, our will and our nature are transformed as
the power and love of Jesus lifts us (see Jas 4:8–10). Let us
look at three beatitudes:

♦ *Blest are they who hunger and thirst for holiness; they
shall have their fill.* Paul is a good disciple to instruct

you about hunger and thirst for holiness. He tells you of his zeal and enthusiasm for the Law. In his zeal he developed an enormous cruelty and pride, leading him to persecute and murder Christians. This religious fanatic experienced Jesus and became a passionate Christian. *Ask Paul how his compass was set right in his hunger and thirst for holiness and how he had his fill.*

♦ *Blest are they who show mercy; mercy shall be theirs.* The crucified Jesus brings this beatitude to life in a wonderful way. While he was still suffering, he asked his Father to forgive his persecutors because they were ignorant of the true nature of their actions. He showed mercy as well to the repentant criminal. In Acts Chapter Seven we read of the example set by Stephen. As he was being stoned, "he fell to his knees and cried out in a loud voice, 'Lord, do not hold this sin against them'" (7:60). To the unbeliever this might sound like "holier-than-thou" posturing. *Dialogue with Jesus and Stephen about their spontaneous desire to forgive their enemies and ask them for help understanding the sincerity of their plea.*

♦ *Blest are the single-hearted for they shall see God.* There is no better example for this beatitude than Mary, Mother of Jesus. She was consistently single-hearted, even in enormously difficult situations. She remained true to her words, "I am the servant of the Lord. Let it be done to me as you say" (Lk 1:38). *Dialogue with her about her steadfast commitment to God's will in her life.*

▲ *Reflection*

These beatitudes are a promise to some and a reality in the life of other disciples. They are a promise on the disciple's horizon as he or she journeys into the heart of God; knowing that change will happen, but not yet able to predict the contours of the process. To other disciples these beatitudes are recognized as a reality in the witness of holy men and women, predecessors and contemporaries, who have demonstrated the power and grace of these beatitudes. In all likelihood, there are signs already visible in each disciple's life that these beatitudes contain a revolution of spirit.

Exercise Fifty-Two
JOYOUS SUFFERING

▲ Scripture

Blest too the peacemakers; they shall be called sons
of God. Blest are those persecuted for holiness' sake;
the reign of God is theirs. Blest are you when they
insult you and persecute you and utter every kind
of slander against you because of me. Be glad and
rejoice, for your reward is great in heaven.
  —Matthew 5:9–12

▲ Summary

Through the beatitudes Jesus is offering us a different kind
of existence. This new life of true happiness and union with
God is considered to be foolishness by most worldly standards. Disciples who are guided by the norms set within the
beatitudes have few natural enemies. They seek peace and
union of hearts. They are often misunderstood because
they seek truth and challenge others to do likewise. They
experience joy even in the midst of suffering.

▲ Session

(20–30 minute duration)
Jesus invites you to participate in his passage of passion,
death, and resurrection. Ask the Holy Spirit to help you
understand that the joy of resurrection can be experienced
in the midst of suffering and rejection.

Making these beatitudes a reality in our lives is God's business. Our part is to petition for these graces with faith-filled
hearts, even when we experience strong resistance in doing
so. Let us look at these beatitudes one by one:

♦ *Blest too the peacemakers; they shall be called sons of
God.* All are God's children, no matter what their race,
religion, or culture might be, and God desires to reign in
everyone's heart. A peacemaker has God's heart and disposition. The disciple's mission is to facilitate God's

loving presence among humans. *How have you been a peacemaker in the past? Where is God calling you to be a peacemaker now? Are there sources of resistance within your heart to the peace God desires for you? How visible is God's love and presence in your discipleship?*

♦ *Blest are those persecuted for holiness' sake; the reign of God is theirs.* Invite into your living room several biblical saints who were genuine examples of this beatitude and dialogue with them: Moses, Jeremiah, John the Baptist and James the apostle (both of whom were beheaded by Herod), Peter, and Paul. *Ask them to help you understand the intimate connection between holiness and suffering for God at the hands of humans.*

♦ *Blest are you when they insult you and persecute you and utter every kind of slander against you because of me. Be glad and rejoice, for your reward is great in heaven.* An application of this beatitude is found in Acts Chapter Five. Dialogue with Peter and the apostles about their experience with the Sanhedrin. Peter and the apostles were obedient to God's will and had to suffer through court proceedings, jailing, scourging, and harassment. Through it all they were "full of joy that they had been judged worthy of ill-treatment for the sake of the Name" (Acts 5:41).

▲ *Reflection*

Acts Chapter Five is a David and Goliath story. The Sanhedrin are powerful. These "uneducated men of no standing" (Acts 4:13) are challenging their authority. The Sanhedrin are determined to eradicate this pesky lot, yet the apostles will not go away. They seem to have power, enthusiasm, phenomenal courage, and freedom of spirit. Nothing, not even sustained harassment, represses their convictions. In all of this they are resilient and joy-filled. Such behavior and mind-set is not common to human nature; it is the result of an outpouring of grace into the human heart.

Exercise Fifty-Three
LIGHT IN DARKNESS

▲ Scripture

You are the light of the world. A city set on a hill cannot be hidden. Men do not light a lamp and then put it under a bushel basket. They set it on a stand where it gives light to all in the house. In the same way, your light must shine before men so that they may see goodness in your acts and give praise to your heavenly Father.

—Matthew 5:14–16

▲ Summary

Jesus sets very high standards of moral conduct. His followers are to be luminous and transparent. There are to be no dichotomies between their private and public lives. Is the fulfillment of such a high standard even feasible? It is not possible if the light Jesus refers to is moral perfection made manifest solely by human endeavor. Jesus is talking about making *his* light shine through the disciple, and anything is possible for God.

▲ Session

(20–30 minute duration)

You seek to incorporate Jesus' desire that you be a light to the world into your life. Ask the Holy Spirit to transform you into a disciple who reflects God's goodness in behavior and speech.

Imagine you are sitting in a room where the darkness is total. You sit in this space for several minutes. Even when your eyes grow accustomed to the darkness, you cannot see. You then begin reciting the following scripture passages, *slowly and repeatedly*. As you do so the light in the room, and in your heart, begins to grow brighter and brighter. When you have gone through each passage, dialogue with Jesus over the sentiments welling up in your heart:

♦ "O Lord, let the light of your countenance shine upon us! You put gladness into my heart, more than when grain and wine abound" (Ps 4:7b–8).

♦ "You indeed, O Lord, give light to my lamp; O my God, you brighten the darkness about me; for with your aid I run against an armed band, and by the help of my God I leap over a wall" (Ps 18:29–30).

♦ "The Lord is my light and my salvation; whom should I fear? The Lord is my life's refuge; of whom should I be afraid?" (Ps 27:1).

♦ "The people who walked in darkness have seen a great light; upon those who dwelt in the land of gloom a light has shone. You have brought them abundant joy and great rejoicing" (Is 9:1–2).

♦ "Rise up in splendor! Your light has come, the glory of the Lord shines upon you. See, darkness covers the earth, and thick clouds cover the peoples; but upon you the Lord shines, and over you appears his glory" (Is 60:1–2).

♦ ". . . Your light must shine before men so that they may see goodness in your acts and give praise to your heavenly Father" (Mt 5:16).

♦ "The eye is the body's lamp. If your eyes are good, your body will be filled with light; if your eyes are bad, your body will be in darkness. And if your light is darkness, how deep will the darkness be!" (Mt 6:22–23).

▲ Reflection

Jesus' call to follow in his footsteps and become like him in all things is gently persistent and divinely feasible. We have been called to be "holy and blameless . . . full of love" (Eph 1:4). In the face of human frailty and wickedness, the trust Jesus places in us to cooperate with his grace is both consoling and encouraging. The disciple's response to God's call rests solely on trust in the Master's voice.

Exercise Fifty-Four
UNCOMPROMISING COMPASSION

▲ Scripture

Be compassionate, as your Father is compassionate. Do not judge, and you will not be judged. Do not condemn, and you will not be condemned. Pardon, and you shall be pardoned. Give, and it shall be given to you. Good measure pressed down, shaken together, running over, will they pour into the fold of your garment. For the measure you measure with will be measured back to you.

—Luke 6:36–38

▲ Summary

Jesus tells us on several occasions that he came not for the just but to answer the needs of sinners. He expresses a special fondness for sinners and seeks their company. While he knows of our human condition better than we do, especially our penchant for sabotaging the good within us, he believes with all his heart that sinners such as ourselves have been called to profound transformation. The purpose of his mission is to bring us salvation and union with God. In accepting discipleship, we also accept Jesus' enthusiasm and optimism for his work in us.

▲ Session

(20–30 minute duration)

Reflect upon your capacity to be as compassionate as God intends. In discipleship, the faithful are called to be non-judgmental and forgiving, a requirement set by Jesus himself. Ask the Holy Spirit to mentor you into being merciful and loving in your interactions with others.

These reflections may help you in your dialogue with Jesus:

♦ *Compassion*—Compassion is the outcome of long and patient reflection on your own pain and suffering. Such reflection engenders a desire to alleviate the sufferings

▼

of others. Compassion is also the result of remorse and sorrow at the realization that your actions have harmed others. Your contrition leads you to want to make amends *How sincere is your suffering?. How do you assess your ability to suffer with others? How deep is your sorrow for the harm you have caused, and what concrete steps have you taken to make amends? Do you make efforts to work on your compassion at all times?*

♦ *No Judgment or Condemnation*—Jesus doesn't ask us to be naive, nor does he ask us to scrutinize the ulterior designs others might have toward us. Jesus' call is a proclamation to surrender pride and ego. *Do you firmly believe that it is God's function to take care of our world? Do you believe your role in God's creation is to love and serve others without frenzy or anxiety?*

♦ *Pardon and you will be pardoned*—God pardons without needing to be pardoned, as only God is without sin. Jesus asks us to pardon because he wants us to be like God, magnanimous and merciful. It does not make sense for us to withhold from another what we ourselves need. Indeed, only patient and compassionate loving can make our world a better place. *Is there anyone whom you have not forgiven? Is there anyone whose pardon you need to ask?*

▲ *Reflection*

St. Francis of Assisi was an ardent believer in the power of compassion and forgiveness. He asked God to make him a channel of divine peace to others. He desired to be God's instrument by treating everyone like divine royalty, serving them with reverence and love. His presence and actions exuded mercy, hope, and the Lord's gift of salvation. No wonder he is as beloved in our present age as he was in his day.

Exercise Fifty-Five
THE OVERFLOWING CUP OF SELFLESSNESS

▲ *Scripture*

He glanced up and saw the rich putting their offerings into the treasury, and also a poor widow putting in two copper coins. At that he said: "I assure you, this poor widow has put in more than all the rest. They make contributions out of their surplus, but she from her want has given what she could not afford—every penny she had to live on."

—Luke 21:1–4

▲ *Summary*

Jesus seems to be making an intimate connection between spiritual freedom and freedom from material possessions. Material possessions are God's gifts to us; we are their caretakers, not their slaves. It behooves us to treat them for our benefit, not our ruin. A foolproof way of knowing that you are truly free of your possessions is to make it a practice every now and then of giving from what you need rather than from your excess. Jesus will recognize you as he recognized the poor widow.

▲ *Session*

(20–30 minute duration)

Jesus invites us to make God our treasure. When God fills our hearts and minds, material possessions play a proper and subordinate role. Ask the Holy Spirit to fill your heart with God's presence. May it be so overwhelming that you come to more fully appreciate that all is gift.

An appropriate way of understanding generosity and selflessness is to visit intimately with some biblical figures and other figures known for their God-centered simplicity of life:

♦ *The poor widow*—This lowly woman received from Jesus what every disciple longs for in their heart. He compliments her with the words: ". . . but she from her want has given what she could not afford—every penny she had to live on." *Dialogue with her about her motivation to give from what she needed to live. Ask what consolations the Holy Spirit produced in her soul as the fruit of her generosity.*

♦ *Barnabas*—Barnabas was an ardent disciple who helped Paul in the earlier stages of his ministry. He is described as "a certain Levite from Cyprus named Joseph, to whom the apostles gave the name Barnabas (meaning 'son of encouragement'). He sold a farm that he owned and made a donation of the money, laying it at the apostles' feet" (Acts 4:36–37). *Dialogue with him about the spirit of generosity and total dedication to God that he shared with the poor widow. How does he reflect on your generosity and selflessness?*

♦ *Francis of Assisi*—Francis was the son of a wealthy merchant and lived early on in leisure and sin. He was immersed in the pleasures and pastimes of the world when he heard the call of the Master. He gave up everything and embraced poverty and simplicity as his lifestyle. God became his only treasure. Francis became a channel of God's peace and love to others. *Talk to Francis about his transformation and seek his advice as to what you need to do in your discipleship.*

▲ Reflection

There is a story about a wandering hermit who shared the spirit of the poor widow, Barnabas, and Francis. He came upon a huge diamond in the road that he put into his begging bag. A brigand waylaid him. The hermit gladly offered him the diamond as the only possession he had. Several days later the robber sought him out to return the diamond. In its place he sought the hermit's secret to peace and joy. He wanted it desperately for himself. As Jesus put it: "Your heavenly Father knows all that you need. Seek first his kingship over you, his way of holiness, and all these things will be given you besides" (Mt 6:32–33).

Exercise Fifty-Six
SERVANT LEADERSHIP

▲ Scripture

It is not ourselves we preach but Christ Jesus as Lord, and ourselves as your servants for Jesus' sake. For God, who said, "Let light shine out of darkness," has shone in our hearts; that we in turn might make known the glory of God shining on the face of Christ. This treasure we possess in earthen vessels, to make it clear that its surpassing power comes from God and not from us.

—2 Corinthians 4:5–7

▲ Summary

Paul has the perfect disposition for a disciple. Jesus Christ saturates his life and ministry. With God's help he has been stripped of his ego. He is an apostle, not for himself, but *only* for Jesus. He has become a servant of the Shepherd and his flock. And he is deeply aware of his own sinfulness and unworthiness. The wonderful treasure that he possesses—the glory of God appearing in the face of Jesus—is contained within him as in an earthen vessel.

▲ Session

(20–30 minute duration)

On numerous occasions both Jesus and the apostles emphasize servant leadership. Ask the Holy Spirit to deepen your appreciation of servant leadership as you seek to follow in your Master's footsteps and wash the feet of the people you serve.

Reflect with Jesus on servant leadership as he demonstrated it at the Last Supper:

"You address me as 'Teacher' and 'Lord,' and fittingly enough, for that is what I am. But if I washed your feet—I who am Teacher and Lord—then you must wash each other's feet. What I just did was to give you an example; as I have done, so you must do. I solemnly assure you, no slave is greater than his master; no messenger outranks the one who sent him. Once you know all these things, blest will you be if you put them into practice" (Jn 13:13–17).

In Luke's account of the Last Supper we are told of a dispute that arose among the disciples as to whom among them was the greatest. Reflect on Jesus' response to them:

"Earthly kings lord it over their people. Those who exercise authority over them are called their benefactors. Yet it cannot be that way with you. Let the greater among you be as the junior, the leader as the servant. Who, in fact, is the greater—he who reclines at table or he who serves the meal? Is it not the one who reclines at table? Yet I am in your midst as the one who serves you" (Lk 22:25–27).

In his letter to the Philippians, Paul asks us to imitate Christ's humility:

Though he was in the form of God, he did not deem equality with God something to be grasped at. Rather, he emptied himself and took the form of a slave, being born in the likeness of men. He was known to be of human estate, and it was thus that he humbled himself, obediently accepting even death, death on a cross! Because of this, God highly exalted him and bestowed on him the name above every other name, so that at Jesus' name every knee must bend in the heavens, on the earth, and under the earth, and every tongue proclaim to the glory of God the Father: Jesus Christ is Lord!" (Phil 2:6–11).

Spend time with Jesus reflecting on your sentiments and ask him to expand and deepen your servant leadership.

▲ Reflection

Saint Ignatius of Loyola identified the path to alienation from God as being the insatiable desire for riches, which leads to a hunger for honor and power, which leads to pride or setting oneself up as the yardstick. The antidote to the way of the world is Jesus' way, which emphasizes poverty or freedom from attachment to material possessions and status. Liberation from the bondage of materialism leads to accepting humiliation and being misunderstood by worldly standards, which leads further to humility or true freedom in God.

Exercise Fifty-Seven
LOVE YOUR NEIGHBOR AS YOURSELF

▲ Scripture

My brothers, what good is it to profess faith without practicing it? Such faith has no power to save one, has it? If a brother or sister has nothing to wear and no food for the day, and you say to them, "Good-bye and good luck! Keep warm and well fed," but do not meet their bodily needs, what good is that? So it is with the faith that does nothing in practice. It is thoroughly lifeless.

—James 2:14–17

▲ Summary

We know from experience how hollow a profession of love sounds when loving acts don't follow. In our relationship with God it is not enough to bask in God's promises of unconditional love. God's providence surrounds us when we perceive it and when we do not. The only authentic way to know whether we appreciate God's compassionate love for us is by reciprocating with our love. God is best served by obeying God's teachings, in this instance the command to love our neighbor as ourselves.

▲ Session

(20–30 minute duration)

Jesus gave us the new rule to live by: love God with all our hearts, minds, and souls, and our neighbor as ourselves. We can't love God without loving our neighbor. Beseech the Holy Spirit to remove the obstacles in you that would thwart your love and service of neighbor.

♦ *Who is my neighbor, Lord?* A lawyer posed this question to Jesus. In reply Jesus told the parable of the Good Samaritan. At the end Jesus asks, "'Which of these three, in your opinion, was neighbor to the man who fell in with the robbers?' The answer came, 'The one who treated him with compassion.' Jesus said to him, 'Then go and do the same'" (Lk 10:36–37). *Talk to Jesus about your resistance to being like the Good Samaritan.*

◆ *Who is my neighbor, Lord?* Here is what Jesus says,

"If you do good to those who do good to you, how can you claim any credit? Sinners do as much. . . . Love your enemy and do good; lend without expecting repayment. Then will your recompense be great. You will rightly be called sons of the Most High, since he himself is good to the ungrateful and the wicked" (Lk 6:33, 35).

◆ *In reflection, assess your life in dialogue with Jesus.*

◆ *Who is my neighbor, Lord?* Here is what Jesus says,

"Be compassionate, as your Father is compassionate. Do not judge, and you will not be judged. Do not condemn, and you will not be condemned. Pardon, and you shall be pardoned. Give, and it shall be given to you. Good measure pressed down, shaken together, running over, will they pour into the fold of your garment. For the measure you measure with will be measured back to you" (Lk 6:36–38).

◆ *What does this teaching mean to you? Ask Jesus to explain!*

◆ *Who is my neighbor, Lord?* Here is what Jesus says,

"How can you say to your brother, 'Brother, let me remove the speck from your eye,' yet fail yourself to see the plank lodged in your own? Hypocrite, remove the plank from your own eye first; then you will see clearly enough to remove the speck from your brother's eye" (Lk 6:42).

◆ *How comfortable are you in acknowledging your own sinfulness in prayer? Ask Jesus to walk with you down this road toward compassion.*

▲ Reflection

We have little difficulty being responsible for loving and taking care of our own. We are even prepared to make great sacrifices for them. Most of us would create a second circle of caring and service in which we would include our extended family, friends, and concerns for the world in general. For the most part, our prayer would be limited to these two intimate circles. Treating those outside these circles as neighbors, even our enemies, is alien to us. Jesus is asking us to treat them as our own.

Exercise Fifty-Eight
TRANSPARENCY OF HEART

▲ Scripture

So strip away everything vicious, everything deceitful; pretenses, jealousies, and disparaging remarks of any kind. Be as eager for milk as newborn babies—pure milk of the spirit to make you grow unto salvation, now that you have tasted that the Lord is good.

—1 Peter 2:1–3

▲ Summary

Peter is aware that the spiritual life cannot be lived on a plateau, with complacency ruling. There is a constant battle within us between the forces of God's light and the forces of evil. Hence the urgent need to be vigilant and practice the art of moral inventory. Peter suggests that we focus on starving our negative tendencies by stripping them away and allowing God's presence to fill our life with goodness.

▲ Session

(20–30 minute duration)

Take a few moments to prepare for your visit with Jesus by asking the Holy Spirit to anoint your mind and heart, so that you are truly transparent to God's ways and designs.

Imagine you are surrounded by a band of disciples who have walked in the Master's footsteps before you. Invite some of these holy people to tell you their story of discipleship. You could include some contemporaries, both men and women. Here are some offerings:

♦ *Peter the Apostle*—Go over the scripture passage he offers you from his letter. Reflect and pray over the meaning of these words.

♦ *John the Beloved Apostle*—The Holy Spirit gave him an understanding of God's mystery that is astounding to the human mind. The Prologue of his gospel is an inspiring passage on which to reflect and pray. The entire body of his collected writings lends itself to personal reflection and meditation.

♦ *Paul the Apostle*—Paul based his entire ministry on one profound experience with Jesus. He also had the enviable ability to communicate God's mystery through the written word. You can choose any passage(s) from his epistles. My favorite is his letter to the Ephesians.

♦ *Matthew the Apostle*—Matthew's gospel tells us a lot about the profound changes Jesus brought into his life. Specifically, given his background as a tax collector, he reflects on the need to be free of preoccupation with riches and honor. Reflect on his calling (Mt 9:9–13); the parable of the Treasure and the Pearl (Mt 13:44–46); and the danger inherent in riches (Mt 19:16–30).

♦ *Luke the Physician*—His gospel and the Book of Acts give us deep insight into this holy man's discipleship. We have much to learn from his example of conscientious discipleship. Consider the parables of mercy in Chapter Fifteen of his gospel and the parable of the Good Samaritan in Chapter Ten.

Spend time with Jesus talking about the movements of the Holy Spirit as they stir your heart. Listen closely as the Spirit guides you.

▲ *Reflection*

As humans we benefit greatly from having role models in our lives that lend support and strengthen us when life's challenges are beginning to swamp us. In the spiritual life it is heartening to belong to the communion of saints, to know that many holy women and men have preceded us in their love and acceptance of Jesus. Their example and prayer can act as a shining beacon on our journey into God's heart. The prayer of grateful remembrance can be a big boost to our discipleship.

Exercise Fifty-Nine
POSSESSING A DISCERNING HEART

▲ Scripture

Beloved, do not trust every spirit, but put the spirits to a test to see if they belong to God, because many false prophets have appeared in the world. This is how you can recognize God's Spirit: every spirit that acknowledges Jesus Christ come in the flesh belongs to God, while every spirit that fails to acknowledge him does not belong to God.
—1 John 4:1–3a

▲ Summary

John warns his Christian communities of divisive and confusing elements in their midst. They are difficult people who claim special knowledge of God but disregard love of neighbor and refuse to accept faith in Christ as the source of sanctification. Thus they deny the redemptive value of Jesus' death. An essential characteristic of Christian discipleship is to constantly test the spirits, and to be guided only by those that acknowledge and lead to Jesus as Savior and Lord.

▲ Session

(20–30 minute duration)
Ask the Holy Spirit to teach you the art and wisdom of discernment, and to help you follow steadfastly the promptings that lead you to God.

In this session peacefully review your spiritual consciousness to see how attuned you are to the workings of the Holy Spirit:

♦ *Review a time in your life when you were in spiritual crisis.* You felt removed from God. Prayer was difficult, you were tepid and slothful, and there seemed to be no desire or urgency to remedy your situation. You were in desolation and consumed by the spirits that were contrary to God's Holy Spirit. You were attracted to what was low and earthly. *Try to become cognizant of the harmful effects such a state of desolation caused in you.*

♦ *Review a time in your life when you were in a state of consolation.* This was a time of renewal and joy. Your perception of God was close and tangible. You were drawn to the holy things of God. Prayer flowed easily and was desirable. You shunned temptation even when it was challenging. *Take your time to appreciate the Holy Spirit's overshadowing of you, and the beneficial effects such a state had on you and others through your good example and efforts.*

♦ *Review a time in your life when you were in a state of spiritual purification.* You longed for God incessantly, yet your desires never seemed to get satiated. God seemed absent, and that dryness increased your thirst for prayer. The frustration lay in the fact that you longed for God, and nothing other than God could truly satisfy you. Yet God was beyond your reach as you walked in the dryness of the desert. *What lessons did you learn, and how did God come to you in such a period?*

♦ *Review a time in your life when you were beset by trials and tribulations from the outside.* Your back was bent double. You continued to trust in God's providence and solicitude for you even though you felt alone and vulnerable. *In hindsight, realize that God was your lifeline, even closer to you than your breath.*

Spend time with the Holy Spirit in thanksgiving for the continual guidance and mentoring you have received in your spiritual life. Express your sorrow for straying from the straight path and once again ask the Holy Spirit to renew your commitment to God's ways and directions in your life.

▲ Reflection

More than a practice or art, discernment is a way of life. When the Holy Spirit holds sway in the disciple's life, the result is transformation into the living image of Jesus.

Exercise Sixty
THE NATURE OF ASSURANCE

▲ *Scripture*

Jesus then said to him: "You became a believer because you saw me. Blest are they who have not seen and have believed."

—John 20:29

▲ *Summary*

So much of life is mystery. The only viable way of handling God's mystery so that it produces wonder and hope is to walk in faith. While an important dimension of faith is to walk in darkness and struggle with questions that have no human answers, an even more significant dimension is the realization that the stumbling walk is made possible by the assurance that God walks with the disciple.

▲ *Session*

(20–30 minute duration)

You seek a special grace from the Holy Spirit, the spiritual insight to understand that the God of consolations does not necessarily come with the consolations of God. As you grapple with that concept, visit the lives of holy men and women who have led the way, going before us. Consider Abraham; Sarah; Moses; Jeremiah; Mary, the mother of Jesus; Joseph, the husband of Mary; and others. These people of God stayed the course even when the consolations of God were taken away from them. God became their Absolute to the point where faithfulness to prayer and God's will transformed their nature, even when they received no tangible or sensible signs of God's love. Five ponderings are posited here for your consideration:

♦ Have you made it a practice to pray immediately for your enemies, both those who harbor resentments against you and those whom you dislike? If not, what kind of prayer would emanate from your reluctance?

- Do you refrain from gossiping, even when you believe that the person deserves to be "put in their place"? Have you visited that "place" to increase your understanding and tolerance?

- When praise and adulation come your way, do you remind yourself how fleeting and fickle human appreciation can be? What does the Lord say we deserve?

- Are you more concerned about loving and serving others than being loved?

- Do you love your Church, the body of Christ, even when parts of the whole disappoint and disillusion you? At the Eucharistic table, do you sense Christ among us? How do you still believe in the power of the risen Lord?

Dialogue with Jesus over your responses to these questions.

▲ Reflection

God's holiness has so inundated the disciple's consciousness that there is no longer the need to question the circumstances of one's life. The disciple no longer needs assurances. God's word is enough. The disciple's very nature has been transformed as God has seen fit. Faith is the disciple's walk. Faith is illumined darkness. In questions, suffering, and pain, the resurrection of Jesus shines. So as you carry on, you go at Godspeed.

CHAPTER GLEANINGS

▲ Without Jesus the disciple's life and ministry are meaningless. Many followers enter into ministry with enthusiasm and fervor because their lives have been touched in dramatic and poignant ways, but, all too often, they slip away from a solid reliance on their true source and sustenance, Jesus. They are like grains of wheat that fall by the wayside, or on rocky ground, or among thorn bushes.

▲ The disciple makes it a practice to live conjointly with Jesus. Everything in the disciple's life is open to scrutiny and supervision by Jesus.

▲ In the face of human frailty and wickedness, the trust Jesus places in us to cooperate with his grace is both consoling and encouraging. The disciple's response to God's call rests solely on trust in the Master's voice.

▲ In the spiritual life, it is heartening to belong to the communion of saints, to know that many holy women and men have preceded us in their love and acceptance of Jesus.

▲ More than a practice or art, discernment is a way of life. When the Holy Spirit holds sway in the disciple's life, the result is transformation into the living image of Jesus.

▲ While an important dimension of faith is to walk in darkness and struggle with questions that have no human answers, an even more significant dimension is the realization that the stumbling walk is made possible by the assurance that God walks with the disciple.

Notes

1. Ken Krabbenhoft, trans., "I Live Without Living In Myself," in *The Poems of St. John of the Cross* (NY: Harcourt, Brace & Company, 1999).

2. Krabbenhoft, "O Living Flame of Love."

ACKNOWLEDGMENTS

The inspiration for writing this book has come from listening to disciples talk about the quiet and wondrous ways in which the Holy Spirit has been working in their lives. Many of these disciples are in Group spiritual direction with me in the Dioceses of Gaylord and Grand Rapids, Michigan. A good number are in Deaconate Formation Programs in the Dioceses of Gaylord and Grand Rapids, Michigan, and Victoria, Texas. Their experiences have warmed my heart and strengthened my spirit. I wish to acknowledge them with gratitude and love.

I wish to acknowledge Cherrie, my wife, who continues to support and encourage my endeavors at proclaiming God's reign through the printed word. Her prayer, presence, and discipleship continue to refurbish my own journey in the Master's footsteps.

I wish to acknowledge some of our special friends: Martha Siwinski who has inspired us by her prayer and love for the Lord, and Susan Thompson who offers us support and inspiration through prayer and shared wisdom.

Ave Maria Press, especially in the person of Bob Hamma, Editorial Director, has continued to be gracious and willing in their support and cooperation with my endeavors. Working with them has been a privilege and joy.

In a special way I wish to thank Bishop Patrick Cooney for his encouragement and support of my endeavors in his Diocese of Gaylord, Michigan, as well as Bishop Robert Rose of Grand Rapids Diocese for his encouragement and solicitude.

Finally, I owe my thanks to our gracious God who uses me as a spokesperson for the Good News. To God be all praise and glory!

Michael Fonseca is the Director of Spiritual Formation for the Diocese of Gaylord, Michigan. Prior to holding this position he was Coordinator of Spiritual Formation at Saint Luke Institute in Silver Spring, Maryland. In addition to designing and executing spiritual formation programs, Fonseca is a licensed professional counselor and an experienced spiritual director and retreat leader. He has given retreats throughout the United States as well as several other countries. His book, *Living in God's Embrace*, was published by Ave Maria Press in 2000. He and his wife, Cherrie, direct a small retreat center from their home in Ravenna, Michigan.